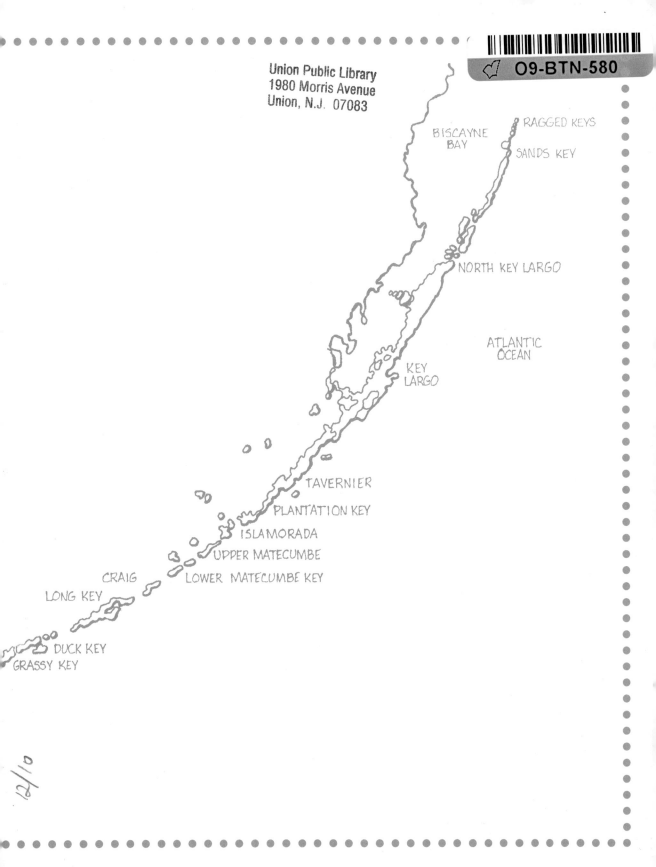

BISCAYNE
BAY

RAGGED KEYS

SANDS KEY

NORTH KEY LARGO

ATLANTIC
OCEAN

KEY
LARGO

TAVERNIER

PLANTATION KEY

ISLAMORADA

UPPER MATECUMBE

CRAIG

LOWER MATECUMBE KEY

LONG KEY

DUCK KEY

GRASSY KEY

12/10

THE *Flavors*
OF THE
Florida Keys

THE *Flavors* OF THE *Florida Keys*

Linda Gassenheimer

Photographs by Sandy Levy / Visual Impact

Atlantic Monthly Press
New York

Published simultaneously in Canada
Printed in the United States of America

FIRST EDITION

For more information and how-to photos, please go to
www.FlavorsoftheFloridaKeys.com

To contact Linda Gassenheimer, please go to www.DinnerInMinutes.com

ISBN-13: 978-0-8021-1953-7

Designed by Charles Rue Woods and Matthew Enderlin

Atlantic Monthly Press
an imprint of Grove/Atlantic, Inc.
841 Broadway
New York, NY 10003

Distributed by Publishers Group West
www.groveatlantic.com

10 11 12 13 14 15 10 9 8 7 6 5 4 3 2 1

To my husband, Harold,
for his love, constant enthusiasm for my work, and support

Contents

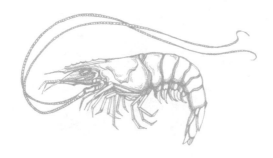

Breakfast

Soups

Main Courses

Salads, Sandwiches, and Side Dishes

Other Keys Desserts

Breads

THE *Flavors*
OF THE
Florida Keys

Introduction

When I wrote my first book about the Florida Keys, *Keys Cuisine*, which was published in 1991, the Keys were a sleepy chain of islands extending out from the mainland of Florida. It was a place reminiscent of the 1950s, where waitresses wore white uniforms and sturdy white laced shoes. There was a lot of good home cooking and the chefs took advantage of the extraordinary local fish. Many years later, I realized that this beautiful cluster of islands extending into the Caribbean Sea has become an even more delectable treasure. Its charming, laid-back atmosphere is still there, but the cuisine is more sophisticated and is served up in a funky, chic ambiance.

Come and travel the Florida Keys with me. Discover hidden treasures off the beaten path; the charm of historic places to eat and the stories of those who created them; and the exciting new wave of international chefs bringing their style of cuisine to restaurants and resorts. You'll meet the Keys characters I came across, who shared their funny stories and tall tales, including local fishing guides and fifth- and sixth-generation Conchs.

Entering the Keys from mainland Florida, I'm always amazed at the beautiful expanse of turquoise and sometimes emerald green waters stretching on both sides of the road. It's a beautiful route with the Atlantic Ocean on one side and the Gulf of Mexico on the other; both can be seen from most of the length of the highway. Leaving the hectic world behind, you enter another world. The Overseas Highway takes you from Key Largo to Key West. It's a 110-mile stretch of U.S. 1 with forty-two bridges linking this island chain. It has been designated an All-American Road, which means it contains multiple qualities that are nationally significant and is considered a destination in itself.

Learning a little about the history of the Keys helped me to understand the roots of its culture and cuisine. For centuries, the Keys have been a haven for pirates, fishermen, artists, writers, rum runners, drug runners, and wealthy bons vivants from all over. The culture is peppered with Americans, Cubans, French, British, and Caribbean islanders, all contributing to a dynamic, regional cuisine, based on the fantastic abundance of fresh fish and shellfish and tropical fruits and vegetables. The Keys still draw people and flavors from all over the world. *The Flavors of the Florida Keys* captures an array of dishes unique to this area.

European influence in the Keys can be traced to the arrival of Ponce de León in 1513. He called this chain of untamed islands Los Martirs, the martyrs. Due to the Keys' prominent position along trade routes, they became a landmark for Spanish ships bringing gold and silver from the New World to the Old.

Loyalists to the crown fled to the Bahamas during the Revolutionary War and then migrated to Key West after the war. English-style cooking and flavors from the Bahamas influence cooking there to this day.

A third wave of migration occurred in 1898 when many Cubans crossed the Gulf Stream to Key West to escape the War of Rebellion with Spain. At one time, they made up one-third of Key West's population, and their influence still plays an important role there.

So what do we find as we discover this magical melting pot? Let's start with Key West, which at one time was the largest city in Florida. As a result of its beautiful natural port, it became a refueling station for ships plying the Caribbean. Today, you can wander on Duval Street and join the party at Sloppy Joe's or Margaritaville or savor the specialties from the many restaurants that line the street. Or, you can explore beyond the main drag and stop at BO's Fish Wagon, a shack built around a wagon cum kitchen, serving some of the best fish sandwiches in town. Just before entering Key West, stop on Stock Island at the Hogfish Bar and Grill for a melt-in-your-mouth fish sandwich made from fish caught that day. Recipes from these restaurants and many more fill the pages here.

Just a two-hour drive from Miami is Duck Key at mile marker 61, where Hawks Cay Resort and Marina is situated. On this secluded island, where the pace of life is a little slower and the sun never takes the winter off, is this tropical retreat. It's spread over sixty palm-lined acres. Originally called the Indies Inn, the resort dates back to the 1950s and was designed by the famed Fontainebleau architect, Morris Lapidus. There have been many changes of ownership, and in 2008 a $35 million renovation turned it into one of the top resorts. Along with the renovation came a team of culinary masters. Try Chef Tony Glitz's Jumbo Shrimp Escabeche or his Dulce de Leche Cheesecake. Their White Sangria has become one of my favorite drinks.

The Upper and Middle Keys have a different character from the Lower Keys, which include Key West. They were settled by farmers and fishermen who made their living from the land and the sea. They planted coconuts, pineapples, tomatoes, citrus, and melons. There were no roads or bridges over the islands, and the only means of transport were shallow draft boats that took their goods to deeper waters where they were reloaded onto schooners. These limitations meant that there was less contact with other cultures and they remained a sleepy backwater.

Several major events turned the Keys into the thriving, vibrant community it is today. Transportation and water were the key elements. First was the advent of Henry Flagler's railroad stretching from the mainland to Key West, completed in 1912. Key West thrived. Fruits and vegetables shipped from the Caribbean and South America were loaded onto trains and transported north. The farmers in the middle keys couldn't compete with the cheaper prices of the imported produce. Competition and overplanting brought an end to plantation farming in the Keys.

Another major event changed the Keys forever. On September 2, 1935, a catastrophic hurricane hit Islamorada and the surrounding Keys. An eighteen-foot tidal wave driven by 250-mile-per-hour winds killed hundreds of people and destroyed the railroad tracks. Key West was cut off from the mainland for three years until a road was built along the railroad tracks. The road was only a partial link; ferries were needed where bridges over the islands were not yet built.

The economy of the Upper Keys was devastated. Searching for a source of income, the locals turned to commercial and game fishing. Small communities grew up around fishing camps. The Key Largo Fisheries grew with them, selling the catch of the day. Jack Hill, just home from the war, opened the fishery with his wife, Dottie. His father was a commercial fisherman. They decided to buy some land and sell their fish. It grew so fast that they started buying fish from other fishermen who would bring whatever they caught that day to earn enough money to go out fishing the next day. Owner Dottie Hill is still there helping her children, who run the fishery now, and today their fish, fresh and frozen, is sold around the world.

Life in the Middle and Upper Keys centered around fishing, drinking, and eating. In 1947, the Green Turtle Inn in Islamorada had a juke box and served local turtle and conch steak. Today, the Green Turtle Inn is still going strong. It's grown into a major center with a restaurant, Wyland Art Gallery, and Keys Outfitters, and still serves local seafood. But back then, looking for more lively entertainment, the locals would go to Plantation Yacht Harbor or Martin's Halfway House where there was a piano and Saturday nights a trio from Homestead on the mainland. There were no drinking-hour restrictions. Jack's Bar was open twenty-four hours a day seven days a week. This was a small community and people trusted one another. During the late fifties and sixties, no one in the Upper Keys locked their doors. When a restaurateur went out with friends, the restaurant was left open, and whoever came in helped themselves to a drink and left their money on the bar.

Once more a major event changed the Keys in 1982, the addition of a new water pipeline. Lack of fresh water had kept the Keys a quiet, sleepy part of America. In 1942 the navy built an eighteen-inch water pipeline that ran 130 miles from Florida City on the mainland to Key West. The water took a week to travel the route. This kept the large developers away. However, in 1982 the old pipeline was replaced with a thirty-six-inch line, increasing the volume of water fourfold. With the access to fresh water came a population boom. Visitors from around the world came to stay in the hotels, weekenders from Miami built homes, and people looking for a sunny, relaxed life settled there. In spite of this, the Keys have kept their special ambiance. The fresh, local fish can't be duplicated. Chefs from around the world bring their own expertise and add the local ingredients for an eclectic, mouthwatering cuisine.

The Flavors of the Florida Keys explores the historic roots with down-home fare and also captures the new more sophisticated culinary treasures. What a delicious adventure as I uncovered recipes from many sources, selecting dishes and drinks that bring the Keys' flavors to life. There are dishes here for every taste that will bring the sunny tropical Keys into your home. Doug Prew and CJ Berwick at The Fish House in Key Largo serve fish from local fishermen and they also have a fish counter and sell it to take home. Meet Raquel Sague Dickson and her brother Mike Sague at Alabama Jack's, a barge just off Card Sound Road in Key Largo for some swinging country music and a goombay smash drink. More chic fare awaits at Hawks Cay Resort and Marina. Try their Mussels with Chorizo in Garlic Sauce or pulled pork made from Sangria Braised Pork. My mouth waters thinking about Key West's Azur's Key Lime Pie French Toast or Pepe's, the oldest eating house in Key West, Coconut Cream Pie. And drink it down with Mrs. Mac's Kitchen's Key Lime Freeze. Join me and enjoy the diverse cultural influences combined with local ingredients that make today's Florida Keys a delicious, tropical corner of the United States. Wishing you all good eating and drinking!

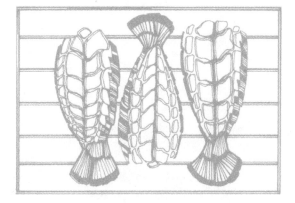

Appetizers and Drinks

Sunset celebrations are always a Keys event. Especially in clearer, cooler weather, they're picture-postcard perfect with their vivid shades of violet, orange, mauve and pink, framed by swaying palm trees.

Life seems to stop as everyone toasts the sunset accompanied by a few snacks and sometimes more substantial appetizers. Mallory Square in Key West is the site of one of the most popular sunset celebrations. It has become more of a circus than anything else, with flame throwers, high-wire acts, arts and crafts booths, and bands playing—to name a few of the attractions. The Keys are a boating paradise, and boaters and their friends often leave the docks to enjoy a sunset cruise. Whether from the deck of a boat, an outdoor terrace, or the patio of a restaurant, it's a special treat to celebrate the sun's descent into the sea.

The drinks in the Keys are delicious and are as pretty as the sunsets. Rum has been the drink ingredient of choice ever since the cultivation of sugarcane and the distillation of "aguardiente," or devil's water. Sugar has been part of Caribbean life since the first sugarcane shoots were brought from the Canaries and planted in Cuba. The rough, killer rum of the sixteenth century became a refined and popular Cuban drink by the middle of the nineteenth century. During Prohibition, according to *Fortune* magazine, "Havana became the unofficial United States' saloon." Airline advertisements read: "Fly to Cuba today and bathe in Bacardi rum." The wide array of rum-based drinks and the varied uses of rum in Keys cooking reflect the popularity of this ambrosia. Today, there are many flavors of rum, from coconut to lemon to orange and more. These flavored rums add a new depth to the drinks in this section.

The Keys appetizers featured in this book are fun, delightful recipes that include such local specialties as Hawks Cay Peel-and-Eat Shrimp with Homemade Cocktail Sauce, Margaritaville's Conch Fritters, and The Fish House's Smoked Fish Dip. More substantial appetizers include Hogfish Ceviche, Island Grill Tuna Nachos, and Square Grouper's Asian-Style Fried Cracked Conch.

Bring a touch of the tropics into your living room. Enjoy these Keys appetizers and drinks and picture the palm trees and sunset for which they were created.

Andrea's Hogfish Ceviche

SERVES 8

You can tell the fish is really fresh when you walk into the Eaton Street Fresh Seafood Market in Key West. There's no fish smell. Andrea Morgan did what many lawyers probably wish they could do: retire at a very young age and move to Key West. She and her husband, Sean Santelli, quickly realized that there were very few fresh seafood markets, despite the fact that they were surrounded by bountiful seas filled with some of the best seafood in the world. In fact, they said, 90 percent of the fish caught here is trekked out of Key West. Sean started fishing on his boat, the *Outcast*, and Andrea started cooking.

Hogfish is a beautifully white firm fish caught in deep water. The texture and flavor, when fresh, are amazing. It's best to assemble the salad just before it is served. Use the freshest fish you can find.

• •

1 orange, freshly squeezed (about 1 cup)
12 limes, freshly squeezed (about 2 cups)
1 tablespoon kosher salt
1 tablespoon hot pepper sauce
1 pound fresh hogfish (grouper or mahimahi can be used)
1 red bell pepper, diced (about 2 cups)
1 small red onion, diced (about 2 cups)
3 plum tomatoes, diced (about 2 cups)
4 celery stalks, with leaves, diced (about 2 cups)
1 small jalapeño pepper, diced
3/4 teaspoon ground white pepper
3/4 teaspoon ground black pepper
1/2 cup cilantro leaves, chopped
Tortillas or crackers for dipping

Juice the orange and enough limes to measure 3 cups. Add the salt and hot pepper sauce to the juice and set aside.

Cut the hogfish into small, bite-size pieces and let marinate in the citrus juice while chopping the red bell pepper, red onion, tomatoes, celery, and jalapeño pepper. Place the vegetables in a large bowl. Spoon the hogfish and all its liquid into the bowl of vegetables. Serve after the hogfish and vegetables have marinated for 30 minutes. The hogfish should be opaque white. Just before serving, stir in the white and black pepper and sprinkle with cilantro. Serve with tortillas or crackers.

Jean Pierre's Ceviche

SERVES 4

Jean Pierre and Diane LeJeune retired from the celebrated Gourmet Diner in North Miami Beach and moved to Islamorada. Jean Pierre didn't retire from cooking, though. He built a large outdoor kitchen with a barbecue, stove, refrigerator, and sink all facing the bay with magnificent views. He still delights in sharing his cooking with friends and family.

His friend Captain Dixon brings him fresh mahimahi and grouper from his daily fishing trips. Jean Pierre says these deepwater, firm, white fish are excellent for ceviche, and he finds that his ceviche is best the next day.

● ●

1 pound mahimahi or grouper
1 red bell pepper
1 sweet onion (Vidalia, red onion), finely sliced
2 medium jalapeño peppers, seeded and chopped
2 cups key lime juice
Large pinch fleur de sel
1 bunch cilantro, chopped leaves only
2 drops Scotch bonnet pepper sauce

Cut the mahimahi into bite-size pieces. Peel the red bell pepper with a potato peeler and cut into julienne strips about 2 inches long and 1/4 inch thick.

Place the fish, red bell pepper, and remaining ingredients in a bowl and stir to mix well. Refrigerate for 8 hours before serving.

Stone Crab and Artichoke Dip

SERVES 8

Andrea Morgan and Sean Santelli, from the Eaton Street Fish Market, take advantage of the local fresh seafood in preparing their dishes. Florida stone crabs are world famous and a favorite of tourists flocking to the area. Andrea lovingly warmed this dip and served it to us.

• •

This dip can be made ahead and stored in the refrigerator for up to three days. It's best served heated. Also, it makes a great stuffing for fish.

> 3/4 cup drained canned artichoke hearts, diced
> 3/4 cup lightly sautéed spinach, well drained and
>   chopped (from 10 cups fresh spinach)
> 3/4 cup mayonnaise
> 3/4 cup freshly grated Monterey Jack cheese
> 3/4 cup freshly grated Parmesan cheese
> 3/4 pound freshly picked stone crab meat (from
>   approximately 2 pounds stone crabs in their shell)*
> 3/4 teaspoon freshly ground sea salt
> 1/4 teaspoon freshly ground white pepper
> 3 tablespoons freshly grated Pecorino Romano cheese

Preheat the oven to 350°F. Stir together the artichoke hearts, chopped fresh spinach, and mayonnaise. Add the Monterey Jack and Parmesan cheeses. Gently stir in the stone crab meat, breaking up any large chunks. Add the salt and pepper. Place in a shallow, oven-proof dish. Sprinkle the Pecorino Romano cheese on top. Place in the preheated oven for 15 minutes or until warm throughout and slightly bubbly. Serve with water crackers.

*Best-quality canned lump crab can also be used.

The Fish House Smoked Fish Dip

SERVES 4

Doug Prew, part owner with CJ Berwick of The Fish House in Key Largo, smokes his own fish very slowly for many hours over buttonwood chips. This wood is very hard and ideal for smoking because it burns slowly and releases generous quantities of heat. His smoked fish has become so popular that people now bring him their fresh-caught fish to smoke. Here's his smoked fish dip.

· ·

1 tablespoon finely chopped onion
1 tablespoon finely chopped celery
1/4 cup softened cream cheese
Several drops Worcestershire sauce
Several drops hot pepper sauce
2 tablespoons seeded, finely chopped jalapeño pepper
4 ounces smoked fish
3 tablespoons sour cream

Mix the onion, celery, cream cheese, Worcestershire sauce, hot pepper sauce, jalapeño pepper, and smoked fish together, breaking up the fish as you stir. Add half the sour cream and taste. Add more sour cream if needed.

Gilbert's Smoked Fish Spread

SERVES 4

Gilbert's Resort and Marina and their Tiki Bar have been part of the Key Largo scene since 1903. Guy Gilbert paid twenty-five dollars for a piece of waterfront property and set up a fishing camp. It's grown into a laid-back resort where they say shoes are optional. Reinhard and Karina Schaupp came from Germany to the Keys to work and decided to buy the resort in 1999. They convinced German restaurateurs Susi and Georg Schu to join them. Georg is the chef and Susi runs the front of the house.

• •

Georg smokes his own fish over hickory chips and juniper berries. He uses mahimahi. You can use any type of smoked fish, except salmon, for this recipe.

> 2 bacon rashers
> 2 ounces cream cheese
> 1/4 cup sour cream
> 2 teaspoons capers, drained
> 1/4 cup diced onion
> 1/4 pound smoked mahimahi
> Crackers or chips for dipping

Cook the bacon until it is crisp. Crumble and add it to the bowl of a food processor or blender. Add the remaining ingredients. Blend until it resembles a smooth pâté. Serve with crackers or chips.

Seafood and Spinach Dip

SERVES 8

Bentley's Restaurant in Islamorada is a family-friendly spot. It's casual but stylish, and the food and service are worth a stop. Chef/owner John Malocsay gave me his favorite seafood dip from the menu. It's a perfect way to start a meal.

It can be made a day ahead and stored in the refrigerator. Bring to room temperature before placing in the oven. Sprinkle the fried onions on just before serving.

2 tablespoons butter, divided use
1/2 tablespoon flour
1/2 cup half-and-half
3/4 cup thawed, frozen, chopped spinach, drained
3/4 cup marinated artichokes, rinsed and drained
1/2 cup onion, diced
1 garlic clove, crushed
1/2 pound peeled shrimp, diced
1 tablespoon lemon juice
Salt and freshly ground black pepper
1/2 teaspoon Old Bay seasoning
1 tablespoon mayonnaise
Several drops hot pepper sauce
1/4 cup shredded Cheddar cheese
1/2 cup canned fried onions
Tortilla chips for dipping

Heat 1 tablespoon butter in a skillet. When melted, add the flour and stir to combine. Add the half-and-half and cook until the sauce is thickened. Make sure the spinach is well drained, and add it to the sauce with the artichoke hearts. Cook to heat through. Set aside.

Heat the second tablespoon of butter in a second skillet over medium-high heat. Add the onion and garlic and sauté until softened, about 2 minutes. Add the shrimp and cook for another minute. Add the lemon juice and the salt and pepper to taste. Add the Old Bay seasoning and stir to combine the flavors. Remove from the heat and stir in the spinach mixture. Add the mayonnaise and hot pepper sauce. Place in an oven-proof dish. (Can be made ahead to this point.) Sprinkle the cheese on top. Preheat the oven to 350°F. Place the dip in the oven and heat until the cheese is melted. Sprinkle the fried onions on top and serve.

Senor Frijoles Salsa

SERVES 4

Senor Frijoles has been serving Mexican food in Key Largo since 1979. A margarita made with fresh lime juice, tortilla chips, and their homemade salsa are perfect companions for enjoying a spectacular Keys sunset at their restaurant facing the Gulf of Mexico.

Senor Frijoles uses *giardiniera*, an Italian condiment of mixed pickled vegetables. You can find it bottled in some supermarkets. Look for pickled vegetables containing cauliflower florets, celery, red bell pepper, olives, and carrots, or a combination of firm pickled vegetables.

● ●

1 1/2 cups drained *giardiniera* vegetables, liquid reserved
1/4 cup chopped onion
1/2 cup diced tomato
2 tablespoons seeded and chopped jalapeño pepper
2 tablespoons key lime juice
Tortilla chips for dipping

Coarsely chop the *giardiniera* vegetables and place in a bowl. Add 2 tablespoons of reserved pickling liquid, the chopped onion, diced tomato, jalapeño pepper, and key lime juice. Mix well. Serve with tortilla chips.

Alma's Jumbo Scallop Escabeche

SERVES 4

Juicy jumbo scallops are sweet and perfect for this dish. They're quickly seared and then marinated in lime juice, white wine, and olive oil. Chef Tony Glitz from Alma Restaurant at Hawks Cay Resort shared his recipe. He told me that one of the reasons he was drawn to the Keys from his native Ontario, Canada, is the availability of fresh shellfish. He loves creating recipes inspired by the location of Hawks Cay in the midst of the best fishing grounds in the Keys, and this one is a palate pleaser.

Escabeche is cooked fish or sometimes meat that is marinated in an acidic sauce, whereas ceviche is raw fish marinated in an acidic sauce.

• •

3 tablespoons olive oil, divided use
12 jumbo or large scallops
1/2 cup carrots, cut into julienne strips (about 1/4 inch
    thick, 2 inches long)
1 cup red onion, cut into julienne strips (about 1/4 inch
    thick, 2 inches long)
1 sprig fresh thyme
1 garlic clove, crushed
1 tablespoon white wine
1 tablespoon lime juice
1 tablespoon red wine vinegar

Heat 1 tablespoon olive oil in a large skillet. Add the scallops and sear for 1 minute. Turn and sear the second side for 1 minute. Add the carrots, onion, thyme, and garlic. Cook for 1 minute. Add the white wine, lime juice, vinegar, and the remaining 2 tablespoons olive oil. Remove from the heat and place in a small bowl, making sure the scallops are covered with the marinade. Refrigerate for 24 hours.

To serve, stand the scallops on end and slice them as thinly as possible to create thin rounds. Place in a circle on 4 plates and spoon a little marinade over them. Place the carrots and onion in the center of the scallop circles and serve.

Buffalo Shrimp

SERVES 4

Ask any of the locals their favorite spots and they often mention small hole-in-the-wall cafés. That's how I found the City Hall Café. It's tucked into a row of buildings near the Islamorada City Hall. Owner John Bedell gave me one of his most popular dishes.

• •

1/2 cup flour
1 pound peeled and deveined jumbo shrimp
1 egg
1 tablespoon milk
3/4 cup panko (Japanese-style bread crumbs)
1/3 cup melted butter
1/2 cup Frank's Red Hot Sauce or any wing sauce
Canola oil for frying
4 celery sticks, cut into 2-inch pieces
1 cup blue cheese dressing

Place the flour in a bowl and add the shrimp. Using a fork to move them, coat the shrimp with the flour. Lightly beat the egg and milk together in a second bowl. Dip the shrimp in the egg mixture and then in the bread crumbs, having placed them in a third bowl, making sure all sides of the shrimp are coated with the bread crumbs. Mix the butter and hot sauce together in a large bowl.

Pour the canola oil into a large saucepan or deep fryer. Heat to 365°F. Add the shrimp and fry for about 2 to 3 minutes or until they are golden. Remove the shrimp with a slotted spoon and drain on a paper-towel-lined plate. Add them to the butter sauce and toss well. Serve the shrimp with the celery sticks and blue cheese dressing.

Tom's Peel-and-Eat Shrimp with Homemade Cocktail Sauce

SERVES 4

Charlotte Miller, the chef at Tom's Harbor House at Hawks Cay Resort, told me she loves to make her own cocktail sauce to go with the sweet, pink Keys shrimp. Her method makes this an easy dish. Have some friends over, cover your table with newspaper, and pile on the shrimp. Imagine you are sitting on the marina in back of Tom's Harbor House, watching the fishing boats as they come in. Charlotte's love of fresh seafood is enhanced by her relationship with the local fishing captains who fish out of the Hawks Cay Marina at her restaurant's doorstep.

• •

Homemade Cocktail Sauce

1/2 cup ketchup
1 teaspoon chili paste (hot pepper sauce can be substituted)
4 teaspoons key lime juice
2 teaspoons prepared horseradish

Place all the ingredients in a bowl and mix well.

Peel-and-Eat Shrimp

1 tablespoon Old Bay seasoning
1 pound large shrimp

Fill the bottom of a steamer with water and add the Old Bay seasoning. Bring to a boil. Place a steaming basket over the water. The bottom of the basket should not touch the water. Rinse the shrimp and place them in the basket. Cover with a lid and steam for 5 minutes. Serve with the cocktail sauce.

Easy-Cook Shrimp with Tomato Key Lime Cocktail Sauce

SERVES 6

Bill Gaiser, owner of the Carriage Trade Garden in Key West, taught me his secret to cooking perfect shrimp every time. I was delighted with the method and I have used it to boil shrimp ever since. Bill has now retired. Here's his fail-safe recipe for cooked shrimp and a simple sauce.

• •

Easy-Cook Shrimp

2 pounds peeled shrimp
1 tablespoon key lime or lemon juice

Rinse the shrimp and place them in a saucepan. Fill the saucepan with enough cold water to completely cover the shrimp. Add the key lime juice. Place the saucepan over medium-high heat and bring the water to a simmer with bubbles just starting around the edge of the pot; the water will start to turn white. Remove the saucepan from the heat and let sit for 1 minute. Drain the shrimp and plunge them into a bowl of ice water. Drain.

Tomato Key Lime Cocktail Sauce

1/2 cup ketchup
1 tablespoon key lime or lemon juice
1/2 teaspoon hot pepper sauce
1 teaspoon Worcestershire sauce

Combine the ingredients in a small bowl and taste for seasoning, adding more Worcestershire or hot pepper sauce if desired. Spoon into a serving bowl and serve with the shrimp. Makes about 1/2 cup sauce.

Island Grill Guava Shrimp

SERVES 4

Years ago, Eastern Airlines pilot Jack McCormick loved to go to the Keys. During one trip, he stopped at a floating restaurant and couldn't get a beer there. Later, he bought the restaurant on a whim, and now it's been voted best overall restaurant in the Upper Keys by People's Choice Awards. Here's one of the reasons why: fresh Keys shrimp served with a guava barbecue sauce.

1 fresh guava (1/2 to 3/4 cup puree)
1 cup ketchup
1 teaspoon blackened seasoning
1 teaspoon Old Bay seasoning
2 tablespoons rice vinegar
10 bacon rashers
20 large shrimp, peeled
20 long wooden skewers
Canola oil for frying

Peel and seed the guava, then puree it in a food processor. Add the ketchup, blackened seasoning, Old Bay seasoning, and rice vinegar. Strain the mixture and transfer it to a saucepan. Bring to a simmer over medium-high heat and cook for 1 to 2 minutes. Set aside.

Cut the bacon rashers in half horizontally. Wrap one piece of bacon around each shrimp. Pierce the bacon and shrimp with a skewer.

Heat the oil in a deep fryer or large saucepan over high heat to 365°F. Add the shrimp and fry for about 1 minute or until the bacon is crisp. Remove the shrimp and drain on a paper-towel-lined plate.

Serve the shrimp on a platter and spoon a little barbecue sauce over them. Serve extra sauce on the side for dipping.

Alma's Shrimp and Avocado Timbale

SERVES 4

Cooked shrimp and ripe avocado make an attractive and easy appetizer using two abundant local ingredients. There's no cooking necessary here. Chef Tony Glitz from Alma Restaurant at Hawks Cay Resort created this recipe.

The chive-oil garnish should be made a day ahead. It will last several days in the refrigerator and can be used to garnish other salads.

● ●

Chive Oil

1/4 cup chives
1/2 cup parsley
1/2 cup olive oil
Pinch salt

Bring a small saucepan filled with water to a boil. Add the chives and parsley. As soon as the water returns to a boil, drain and rinse the herbs in cold water. Drain and place on a paper towel to dry. Add the herbs and oil to a blender. Blend for several seconds until the oil is green. Line a strainer with a coffee filter or several paper towels and set it over a bowl. Add the chive oil and let drain overnight to remove all of the particles. Set aside.

Shrimp and Avocado Timbale

30 cooked, peeled medium shrimp
1 cup diced ripe avocado (about 1 small avocado)
1/2 cup chopped red onion
1/2 cup chopped cilantro
1/2 cup diced red bell pepper
4 tablespoons lime juice

Mix the shrimp, avocado, onion, cilantro, red bell pepper, and lime juice together. Spoon into 4 molds or ramekins about 4 inches in diameter and 1 1/2 inches deep.

To serve, unmold the timbales onto 4 plates and drizzle chive oil around the edge of the plates.

Shrimp with Ginger Lemon Glaze

SERVES 4

Sitting on the porch at Santiago's Bodega, I looked out on the Bahamian Village area of Key West. It consists of little houses on narrow streets with an architectural style harking back to the origins of Key West. This charming spot is off the beaten track, but word of mouth brings a steady stream of visitors, including celebrities like Jimmy Buffet. In fact, so many people come looking for the restaurant that local owners have posted a sign: "Santiago's—One Block."

I tasted a sweet and citrusy shrimp cocktail there. The dish is made with Key West pink shrimp. This shrimp is plump and juicy. They're pink when raw. Use best-quality shrimp for this recipe.

● ●

5 1/3 cups water
4 cups rice wine vinegar
3/4 cup lemon juice
3 tablespoons powdered ginger
1/4 cup lime zest
4 teaspoons crushed red pepper
1/4 cup cornstarch
1 cup water
20 cooked shrimp
1/4 cup chopped fresh cilantro

Place 5 1/3 cups water, the rice vinegar, lemon juice, powdered ginger, lime zest, and crushed red pepper in a saucepan. Bring to a boil. Mix the cornstarch in 1 cup water in a small bowl. Add to the saucepan and bring back to a boil over high heat. Cook until the glaze is thickened. Place the shrimp on a small dish and spoon the glaze on top. Sprinkle with chopped cilantro.

Ballyhoo's Grilled Oysters

SERVES 4

The historic building that houses Ballyhoo's Restaurant was originally part of a fishing camp in the 1930s. The Florida Keys became known for its sportfishing at that time. It's one of the few original Keys buildings still in use. One reason is that it's made out of Dade County pine, a wood so strong that you have to use screws when building with it. The buildings made out of this special wood have withstood many storms, starting with the catastrophic hurricane that hit the Upper Keys in 1935 .

• •

Grilling oysters with wine and garlic butter complements their fresh flavor.

> 1/2 pound butter, at room temperature
> 4 garlic cloves, crushed
> 24 oysters, opened and drained
> 1/2 cup chardonnay wine
> 1 tablespoon chopped parsley
> Salt and freshly ground black pepper to taste

Preheat a barbecue or stove-top grill. Whip the butter and garlic together. Place the oysters in a roasting pan or tray. Pour the wine over the oysters and top with the garlic butter. Place the oysters on the grill grates and close the grill. If using a stove-top grill, cover them with a lid. Grill for 10 to 12 minutes. Sprinkle the parsley over the oysters. Divide the oysters among 4 plates and serve immediately.

Cedar-Smoked Scallops with Pineapple Chimichurri Sauce

SERVES 6

The famed Cheeca Lodge has been part of Islamorada history since the early 1940s. It's been through many changes and renovations. After a major renovation in 2008, the resort had a fire on December 31, 2008. It has been completely rebuilt, keeping its classic Florida architecture and its spirited tradition of "barefoot elegance."

Chef de Cuisine David Matlock created this recipe. He said it was not too fussy but uses great island-inspired ingredients that are fresh and delicious. Chimichurri sauce is usually made with cilantro, parsley, garlic, vinegar, and oil. The addition of pineapple juice gives this one a sweet and tangy flavor.

• •

3 small cedar planks or 1 large one
1/2 cup pineapple juice
1 cup fresh parsley
1 cup fresh cilantro
2 tablespoons diced red onion
1 tablespoon rice vinegar
1/4 cup olive oil plus 1 tablespoon, divided use
Salt and freshly ground black pepper to taste
18 large scallops

Soak the cedar planks in water for several hours. Remove them from the water and char on an outdoor grill or stove-top grill by heating the grill and placing the planks on the hot grill for about 5 minutes or until they start to char.

Preheat the oven to 350°F. Heat the pineapple juice in a saucepan over high heat. Reduce the liquid by half or to measure 1/4 cup. Place the parsley, cilantro, onion, reduced pineapple juice, and rice vinegar in the bowl of a food processor. Process to a paste. Add the 1/4 cup olive oil and continue to process to a sauce. Set aside.

Heat the remaining 1 tablespoon olive oil in a large skillet over high heat. Season the scallops with salt and pepper to taste. Place them in the skillet and sear on both sides, about 2 minutes per side or until golden brown. Place the scallops on the charred wooden planks and set the planks in the oven for about 2 minutes. Remove them from the oven and divide among 6 plates. Spoon the chimichurri sauce over the top.

Sundowners' Crab Cakes with Pommery Mustard Sauce

SERVES 4

Arrive by boat or by car and enjoy a delicious lunch or dinner at this Key Largo treasure. When I tasted Sundowners' crab cakes, I couldn't believe how light and flavorful they were. These are loaded with crabmeat just loosely held together by a mayonnaise-mustard mixture. Manager Paul White gave me their simple secret. They use the best-quality, lump crabmeat and very little filling.

• •

1 egg
2 teaspoons Worcestershire sauce
2 tablespoons mayonnaise
1 teaspoon lemon juice
1 tablespoon Dijon mustard
1 tablespoon melted butter
1 teaspoon Old Bay seasoning
1/2 cup bread crumbs
1 pound jumbo lump crabmeat
2 tablespoons canola oil

Preheat theoven to 350°F. Mix the egg, Worcestershire sauce, mayonnaise, lemon juice, mustard, butter, Old Bay seasoning, and bread crumbs together by hand in a large bowl. Mix in the crabmeat. Form into 4 crab cakes, about 3 to 4 inches in diameter. Heat the oil in a large skillet over medium-high heat. Add the crab cakes. Sauté for 1 minute. Turn and sauté for 1 minute more. Place in the oven for 2 minutes. While the crab cakes bake, mix the sauce.

Pommery Mustard Sauce

1/4 cup whole-grain or coarse-grain mustard
6 tablespoons heavy cream
Salt and freshly ground black pepper to taste

Mix the sauce ingredients together. Spoon onto 4 plates and place the crab cakes in the sauce.

Margaritaville Conch Fritters with Cajun Rémoulade

SERVES 4

Step into Margaritaville on Duval Street in Key West for some of the best live music in town as well as great margaritas, conch fritters, and, of course, cheeseburgers. Jimmy Buffet went to Miami for a booking date. When he arrived there was no job. He found his way to Key West and the seeds for Margaritaville were planted. It opened in 1987 and quickly became the flagship location as Margaritaville expanded.

1 pound ground conch
1/2 cup chopped red bell pepper
1 cup diced onion
4 seeded, chopped jalapeño peppers
1 3/4 cups pancake mix
1/4 cup milk
2 teaspoons kosher salt
1 teaspoon powdered garlic
2 teaspoons Worcestershire sauce
1 teaspoon Old Bay Seasoning
Pinch cayenne pepper
Pinch white pepper
Canola oil for frying

Combine all the ingredients in a large bowl. The batter should be thick and slightly moist. If it is too wet, add a little more pancake mix; or, if too dry, add a little more milk. Refrigerate for at least 1 hour before frying. May be made ahead to this point.

To fry the fritters, heat the oil in a large pot to 365°F. Drop rounded tablespoons of batter into the oil. Fry until golden brown. Serve immediately with Cajun Rémoulade sauce for dipping.

Cajun Rémoulade

1 cup mayonnaise
1 1/2 tablespoons Creole or coarse-grain mustard
1 tablespoon roasted red peppers, chopped
1 tablespoon scallions, finely chopped
1/4 teaspoon blackened seasoning
1/4 teaspoon chili powder
1/4 teaspoon kosher salt
1 tablespoon water

Mix all the ingredients together in a bowl.

Flash-Fried Conch with Ponzu and Wasabi Drizzle

SERVES 4

"Square Grouper has the best fried conch," several people told me. And they were right. Lynn Bell moved from Vermont to the Keys and opened her Square Grouper restaurant in Cudjoe Key at MM 22.5. The restaurant plays on the words *square grouper*, an old Keys reference to bales of marijuana floating in the water. Her T-shirts read, "Square Grouper gone green — Smoked, Baked, and Fried." The plates are square, and the tablecloths are brown butcher paper on square tables, but her food is anything but square. It's delicious.

Her fried conch is served in strips with a coulis of ponzu sauce and a drizzle of wasabi cream. Conch can be very tough, and Lynn says to be sure to remove the skin and beat it hard. You will be able to feel the difference; it will be softer to the touch. She also cuts the conch in half horizontally. After cutting and pounding, the conch should be about 1/4 to 1/2 inch thick.

Use the ponzu sauce recipe here, or you can buy bottled ponzu sauce in many supermarkets.

• •

Ponzu Sauce

6 tablespoons sugar
1/4 cup soy sauce
1/4 cup pineapple juice
1/4 cup orange juice (freshly squeezed, if possible)
2 tablespoons crushed pineapple
2 tablespoons black and white sesame seeds
    (or all white seeds), toasted
Pinch white pepper

Place the sugar, soy sauce, pineapple juice, orange juice, and crushed pineapple in a saucepan. Bring to a boil and stir to dissolve the sugar. Meanwhile, toast the sesame seeds in a toaster oven for 2 to 3 minutes, watching to make sure they don't burn. Remove the sauce from the heat and add the sesame seeds and white pepper. Serve at room temperature.

Wasabi Cream

1/4 cup sour cream
1 tablespoon wasabi powder (or 2 tablespoons
   prepared horseradish)
3/4 tablespoon lemon juice
1 tablespoon milk, if needed
Salt and freshly ground black pepper to taste

Place the sour cream, wasabi powder, and lemon juice in a bowl. Whisk to blend. Season with salt and pepper. Add milk to thin, if necessary. It should be a drizzle consistency.

Conch

1 pound conch
1/4 cup flour
1 egg, slightly beaten
1 cup panko (Japanese-style bread crumbs)
2 medium cucumbers
Canola oil for frying

If there is any skin, remove it. Cut the conch in half horizontally. Cover with plastic wrap and pound with a meat mallet or the bottom of a heavy skillet until the conch softens. Try not to make holes in the conch. Place the flour on a plate, the egg in a bowl, and the bread crumbs on a separate plate. Dip the conch in the flour, then in the egg mixture, and finally in the bread crumbs. Heat the oil in a deep fryer or saucepan to 350°F. Fry the conch for about 1 to 2 minutes or until golden. Drain on a plate lined with paper towels. Cut into 1/4 inch strips. Peel the cucumbers and cut them into thin strips with a zester. To serve, spoon ponzu sauce onto 4 plates. Place the conch strips on the sauce and drizzle wasabi cream on top. Garnish with cucumber strips on the side.

Cobia Crudo

SERVES 4

The Morada Bay Beach Club is next to Pierre's Restaurant. Both are situated on a beautiful beach on the Gulf of Mexico in Islamorada. Morada Bay features open-porch dining right on the beach with top-quality food. Chef David Peck says the sunset views are spectacular, and he uses all local seafood.

Cobia is a large warm-water fish that rates among the best in taste and texture. It is a highly sought-after game fish. Any type of sushi-quality, firm, white-flesh fish can be used.

● ●

1 cup thinly sliced fennel
1/4 cup lime juice, divided use
4 teaspoons sugar
1 orange, juiced
2 garlic cloves, peeled
4 inches fresh ginger, peeled and sliced
1/2 pound fresh cobia
Salt and freshly ground black pepper to taste
1/2 cup micro basil (small, baby basil)

Place the fennel in a bowl and add 8 teaspoons lime juice and the sugar. Toss well and marinate for 15 to 20 minutes.

Place the remaining 4 teaspoons lime juice and the orange juice in a blender. Add the garlic and ginger. Blend until smooth.

Thinly slice the cobia and divide among 4 plates. Spoon the sauce from the blender over the fish. Remove the fennel from the marinade and spoon on top of the sauce. Sprinkle salt and pepper and basil on top.

Island Grill Tuna Nachos

SERVES 4

Island Grill's Jack McCormick mentioned that his Tuna Nachos outsell everything else on the menu. Sushi-grade ahi tuna tops wakame seaweed for this dish. His restaurant is one of Islamorada's most popular stops, and this dish is one of the reasons.

Wakame seaweed can be found dried. It's thin and dark green and adds texture and flavor to salads and soups. Look for it at specialty or health food stores. Seaweed salad found in the supermarket sushi case works well in this recipe. Jack suggests using thinly sliced or shredded lettuce as a substitute.

. . . .

1 pound wakame
1/2 cup balsamic vinegar
1/2 cup low-sodium soy sauce
Canola oil for frying
12 wontons
1 tablespoon wasabi powder
    (horseradish can be used instead)
3 tablespoons mayonnaise
1 3/4 pounds ahi or sushi-grade tuna,
    cut into 1/4-inch cubes
1 1/2 tablespoons black sesame seeds
1 1/2 tablespoons white sesame seeds
4 scallions, sliced

Soak the wakame in water to cover for 10 minutes, or until tender. Rinse and place in boiling water for a few seconds. Immediately plunge into ice water to set the green color. Slice into thin strands, cutting away any thick ribs.

Mix the balsamic vinegar and soy sauce together in a saucepan, place over high heat, and reduce by half. Let cool and then toss the seaweed in the sauce. Set aside.

Heat the canola oil in a deep fryer or large saucepan to 365°F. Add 2 wontons at a time and fry until golden. Place on a paper-towel-lined plate to drain.

Mix the wasabi powder with the mayonnaise and set aside.

Place 3 fried wontons on each of 4 plates. Divide the wakame into four portions and spoon over the wontons. Divide the tuna into four portions and spoon onto the seaweed. Drizzle wasabi mayonnaise over the tuna and sprinkle with the sesame seeds and scallions.

Beer-Steamed Mutton Snapper

SERVES 4

So many people have found the charm of the Florida Keys irresistible. Josh Ardis was no exception. He came for a job opportunity that didn't come through. He found Hawks Cay Resort and Marina and is now a captain on *Tailwalker 2*. He goes fishing every day but still finds time to cook the fish he's caught in the evening. Here is his Beer-Steamed Mutton Snapper, which he told me amazes his friends, who love cutting into it. Any type of whole snapper can be used (hogfish, yellowtail, red snapper). The fish sits over a beer can in the oven. It should be no larger than 8 pounds.

• •

1 whole snapper, about 2 to 3 pounds
1 lemon, sliced
1 can beer
1/2 cup diced tomato
1/2 cup onion, diced
1/2 cup diced green bell pepper

Preheat the oven to 350°F. Ask for the fish to be slit from gill to tail and cleaned. Do not cut through belly. Score the fish in a crosshatch pattern on both sides. Cut the lemon slices in half and stick them, skin side up, in the slits.

Pour the beer from the can into a pitcher or bowl and cut the can in half horizontally. Place the bottom half of the can in a roasting pan and fill it 2/3 with beer. Add some of the tomatoes, onion, and bell pepper to the beer until the can is filled and place the remaining vegetables in the roasting pan. Pour the remaining beer into the pan. Hold the fish upright with the long slit on the bottom. Open the slit in the fish and place it over the can so that the can fits into the cavity. Carefully place the roasting pan in the oven and cook for 20 minutes. The fish is cooked when the flesh flakes easily.

Lift the fish from beer can and lay it on a platter. Pour all the vegetables and beer over the fish. Serve the fish family style, with each person taking a square from the crosshatch design.

Tiki John's Rum Runner

SERVES 1

T he smell of the salt air, the uninterrupted ocean view, and the gentle tropical breeze made the perfect setting for John and Lois Ebert's Tiki Bar. They came to the Keys in 1971 and started managing the Tiki Bar at the Holiday Isle Hotel in 1972. Tiki John became one of the favorite bartenders of the Middle Keys, and the Tiki Bar, with its old thatched roof and driftwood furniture, became famous. The *Chicago Daily News* listed it as one of the top ten bars in the world at that time. John has retired, but the Tiki Bar is still there overlooking the water and is still part of the resort.

John and Lois started out by running a do-it-yourself bar. John would set miniature bottles of liquor on the bar with many kinds of condiments and mixes. You bought a cup and some ice and then went and made your own drink. People started flooding the bar. It was hard to find a place to dock your boat on a nice weekend, and if you were the first one in, you couldn't get out. Soon the Eberts were so busy that they couldn't wait for customers to make their own drinks, and they started bartending themselves.

At that point, John realized that he had inherited too much inventory from the previous manager — his storeroom had too much banana liqueur and blackberry brandy. He mixed these together with some rum and key limes and invented the famous Rum Runner. Tiki John's Rum Runner is a happy drink that is served all over the Keys. Here is John's original recipe.

• •

7/8 ounce blackberry brandy (roughly half a jigger*)
7/8 ounce banana liqueur (roughly half a jigger*)
3/4 ounce 151 rum
1 1/2 ounces grenadine
1 1/2 ounces lime juice (key lime if possible)

To make a frozen drink, fill a blender container 1/3 full with cracked ice or small ice cubes. Add the ingredients and blend until smooth. Serve in a 12-ounce glass.

Or, place all the ingredients in a shaker half filled with ice. Shake well and strain into a 12-ounce glass with several ice cubes in it.

*A jigger is a small cup used by bartenders to pour exactly 1 1/2 ounces of alcoholic spirits. It's standard equipment in most bars.

Hawks Cay's Alma's Rich Sangria

SERVES 4 TO 6

Alma Restaurant at Hawks Cay Resort on Duck Key serves this refreshing sangria. It's perfect for their Latin-inspired menu and refreshing on a warm evening. Enjoy its deep, rich, fruity flavor on its own or with almost any dish.

• •

1 cup fresh berries (strawberries, raspberries, or
    blackberries)
1/4 cup sugar
1 bottle dry red wine (rioja, merlot, Chianti, shiraz)
1/3 cup orange juice
1/3 cup brandy
1/2 green apple, cored and cut into small cubes
2 orange wedges
2 lemon wedges
2 lime wedges
1 cinnamon stick
3 whole star anise
Allspice for sprinkling

Place the berries in a bowl and add the sugar. Set aside while assembling the other ingredients. Pour the wine, orange juice, and brandy into a large pitcher. Add the apple, orange, lemon, and lime wedges, berries, cinnamon stick, and whole star anise. Sprinkle allspice on top. Refrigerate for 2 hours before serving.

Hawks Cay's Alma's Sangria Blanco

SERVES 4 TO 6

A cool glass of sangria is perfect for a warm evening. The Alma restaurant at Hawks Cay Resort on Duck Key serves this unique one. The beauty of this white wine sangria is that it is as delicious as it is easy to make, and it only gets better as you add your favorite fruits!

1 bottle white wine (Riesling, Albariño, Chablis,
  Gewürztraminer, Pinot Gris, chardonnay,
  sauvîgnon blanc)
2/3 cup white sugar
1 orange, sliced
1 lemon, sliced
1 lime, sliced
2 cups mixed fruit, such as raspberries, blueberries, melon,
  pineapple, strawberries (or any combination,
  all cut into small cubes or sliced)
2/3 cup lychee liqueur
1/2 cup white rum
Ginger ale or cava

Pour the wine into a pitcher and add the sugar, orange, lemon, lime, fruit mixture, lychee liqueur, and white rum. Refrigerate overnight. When ready to serve, mix well to evenly distribute the fruit and ladle into a glass half filled with ice. Top off with cava or ginger ale.

The Bar at Alma, Hawks Cay Resort

Fun, funky, and sophisticated is how I describe the Bar at Alma at the Hawks Cay Resort on Duck Key. The drinks are unusual, pretty, and very tasty. You can look out on the bay or enjoy the elegant inside setting. Scott Benton prepared these drinks for us. What a treat!

EACH RECIPE SERVES 1

Little Red Dress

This drink is served in a champagne flute and is a bright red color.

> 2 tablespoons sugar plus 1 1/2 teaspoons
> 10 fresh raspberries
> 2 ounces raspberry-flavored vodka
> Splash rose champagne

Wipe one raspberry around the edge of a champagne flute. Place 2 tablespoons sugar on a plate and dip the glass into the sugar to form a ring of sugar around the edge. Muddle the remaining 1 1/2 teaspoons sugar and 6 raspberries in a shaker. Crush with a muddling stick or use the back of a spoon against the side of the shaker. Add the vodka and fill the shaker with ice. Shake well to dissolve the sugar. Strain into the champagne flute. Add a splash of rose champagne. Add the 3 remaining raspberries as a garnish.

Raspberry Lemonade Fizz

> 2 teaspoons sugar
> 3 lemon wedges
> 6 raspberries
> 2 ounces raspberry-flavored vodka
> 5 ounces lemon/lime soda

In a cocktail shaker, muddle the sugar, lemon wedges, and raspberries. Crush with a muddling stick or use the back of a spoon against the side of the shaker. Add ice and the vodka. Shake well and strain into a 12-ounce glass. Fill the glass with lemon/lime soda.

Special Cay

1 ounce gin
1/2 ounce ginger liqueur
1/2 ounce pomegranate liqueur
Splash fresh grapefruit juice
Splash cranberry juice
1 lime slice

Fill a shaker with ice. Pour in the gin, ginger liqueur, pomegranate liqueur, a splash of grapefruit juice, and a splash of cranberry juice. Shake well. Strain into a martini glass. Float the slice of lime on top.

Snowbird

2 tablespoons chocolate sauce
1 scoop vanilla ice cream
1 ounce vanilla vodka
1/2 ounce white chocolate liqueur
1/2 ounce light crème de cacao

Swirl the chocolate sauce inside a martini glass from top to bottom. In a blender mix together the vanilla ice cream with the vanilla vodka, white chocolate liqueur, and crème de cacao. Pour into the prepared martini glass.

Piña Colada

SERVES 1

Rum, pineapple, and coconut are three tropical ingredients that were made for each other. Put them together and you have one of the Keys' most famous drinks, the Piña Colada.

• •

2 or 3 small fresh pineapple cubes
2 ounces Coco López cream of coconut
1 1/2 ounces light rum
1 1/2 ounces unsweetened pineapple juice
1 ounce dark rum
1/2 slice fresh pineapple
1 maraschino cherry

For a frozen drink, mix the pineapple cubes and coconut cream together in the container of a blender. Half fill the container with cracked ice or small ice cubes. Add the light rum and pineapple juice. Blend until smooth. Pour into a 12-ounce glass. Float the dark rum on top. Place the pineapple slice and maraschino cherry on a long toothpick. Balance on the edge of the glass.

Or, pour all of the ingredients into a shaker half filled with ice. Shake and strain into a 12-ounce glass with several ice cubes in it.

Miami Vice

SERVES 2

Swirling a piña colada and rum runner together produces a popular drink at many Keys bars. The sweetness of the piña colada and the tartness of the rum runner blend beautifully as do the two contrasting colors. At the Hawks Cay Resort's Beach Grill Bar it's called Miami Vice. At other Keys bars it's called Candy Cane or PITA (Pain in the Ass). Make each drink separately and then swirl them together.

• •

Start with the frozen Rum Runner (p. 49) and frozen Piña Colada (p. 54). Spoon some of the Rum Runner into two 12-ounce glasses. Spoon some of the Piña Colada on top. Continue to layer the drinks to fill the glasses. Swirl the drinks in the glass with a spoon or swizzle stick and serve.

Alabama Jack's Key Largo

Looking for a piece of the old Florida Keys? Come to Alabama Jack's on Card Sound Road in Key Largo for great country western music and to watch the clog dancers with their cinched waists, hooped skirts, and lots of petticoats. You can even join in the dancing. Jack and Alice Stratham from Montgomery, Alabama, bought a barge in 1947 and turned it into a gold mine. Phyllis Saque, a single mom, bought it in 1981, raised three children there, and sent them all to college. Her daughter, Raquel, and son, Mike, are back helping to run the successful barge restaurant. Savor a little of Alabama Jack's with these drinks.

EACH RECIPE SERVES 1

AJ's Goombay Smash

1 ounce white rum
1 ounce coconut-flavored rum
4 ounces pineapple juice
Pineapple wedge as garnish

Mix the rums together in a 12-ounce glass. Add enough ice and the pineapple juice to fill the glass. Mix well. Place the pineapple wedge on the rim of the glass as a garnish.

AJ's Parrot Breeze

1 ounce white rum
1 ounce coconut-flavored rum
2 ounces pineapple juice
2 ounces cranberry juice
Orange slice as garnish

Mix the rums together in a 12-ounce glass. Add ice, the pineapple juice, and the cranberry juice to fill the glass. Mix well. Place the orange slice on the rim of the glass as a garnish.

Elena's Cuban Mojito

SERVES 1

Elena Spottswood served these Cuban mojitos at a dinner for the symphony in Key West. They were a hit. "We make them strong, but they're good and refreshing," she told me. Good food and drink run in the Spottswood family. Her mother-in-law, Mary Spottswood, was known for her wonderful Key West parties and excellent food.

Some historians contend that African slaves who worked in the Cuban sugarcane fields during the nineteenth century were instrumental in this cocktail's invention. Guarapo, the sugarcane juice often used in mojitos, was a popular drink among the slaves, who helped coin the name of the sweet nectar. The mojito was a favorite drink of Ernest Hemingway.

• •

8 mint leaves
2 ounces fresh lime juice
2 ounces simple syrup*
2 ounces white rum
Splash club soda
Lime slice and mint sprig for garnish

Place the mint leaves in a long, 12-ounce mojito glass (often called a "Collins" glass), along with the lime juice and simple syrup. Gently mash the mixture with a muddler. The muddler should have a flat end to release the oils from the mint. (A spoon against the side of the glass can be used.) Add the rum and stir. Half fill the glass with crushed ice and then add the club soda. Garnish with the lime slice and mint sprig.

*Many tropical drinks call for simple syrup. It's made by mixing equal amounts of sugar and water together (1/4 cup water and 1/4 cup sugar). Dissolve the sugar in the water and then boil for 3 minutes. The liquid should remain clear. Cool and store in the refrigerator. It will keep for several weeks.

Watermelon Mojito

SERVES 1

The Zane Grey Long Key Lounge is much more than a bar. Zane Grey was the first American millionaire novelist. He was also an avid sport fisherman. The lounge is filled with displays of his gear and original manuscripts. It's also a great place for cocktails overlooking the bay. Here is one of their unusual drinks.

• •

1 1/2 ounces melon-flavored rum
Splash simple syrup*
2 sprigs fresh mint
Splash lime juice
Club soda
1/3 ounce Midori melon liqueur

Add the rum, simple syrup, and mint to a 12-ounce glass. Muddle the mint in the bottom of the glass (crush the mint with a rounded spoon or a mortar). Add enough ice to half fill the glass. Add a splash of lime juice and top the glass with club soda. Add the Midori liquor as a floater on top.

*Many tropical drinks call for simple syrup. It's made by mixing equal amounts of sugar and water together (1/4 cup water and 1/4 cup sugar). Dissolve the sugar in the water and then boil for 3 minutes. The liquid should remain clear. Cool and store in the refrigerator. It will keep for several weeks.

Key Lime Mojito

SERVES 1

Marker 88 is a Keys standby dating back to the 1960s when it was started by Andrew Mueller, who brought his European culinary background to the Keys. The restaurant is now owned by the Stoky family, who keep his tradition going.

The Marker 88 grass-roofed tiki bar overlooks the bay in Islamorada. Sitting there watching the gulls and blue water and sipping their Key Lime Mojito is like being in paradise. The bartender told me this is one of the most popular drinks they serve.

• •

1 1/2 ounces key-lime flavored rum
1 1/4 ounces lime juice
6 to 7 fresh mint leaves
1 tablespoon simple syrup*
Splash club soda

Pour the rum and lime juice into a 12-ounce glass. Add the mint leaves and gently mash with a muddler. The muddler should have a flat end to release the oils from the mint. (A spoon against the side of the glass can be used.) Add the simple syrup and stir. Fill the glass with ice and add a splash of club soda.

*Many tropical drinks call for simple syrup. It's made by mixing equal amounts of sugar and water together (1/4 cup water and 1/4 cup sugar). Dissolve the sugar in the water and then boil for 3 minutes. The liquid should remain clear. Cool and store in the refrigerator. It will keep for several weeks.

Hog's Breath Saloon Key West

J erry Dorminy created the Hog's Breath Saloon in Fort Walton Beach, Florida, as a watering hole for his fishing friends. The Key West branch was opened in 1988. "Hog's breath is better than no breath at all" is a modified version of an expression he remembers from his grandmother.

The good times were rolling when I walked into the Hog's Breath Saloon on Front Street in Key West. The band was playing bluegrass and the drinks were flowing. Jeff Wells, the bartender, didn't miss a beat while he made me these "only in Key West" drinks.

EACH RECIPE SERVES 1

Hogarita

1 1/2 ounces tequila
3/4 ounce orange liqueur
Scant 1/4 ounce orange juice
Splash Rose's lime juice
Sour or margarita mix
Salt

Add ice to a shaker. Pour the tequila, orange liqueur, orange juice, and Rose's lime juice into the shaker and fill the shaker with margarita mix to reach 8 ounces. Wet the rim of a margarita glass and dip it into salt. Shake the liquid mixture and strain into the glass. Garnish with a twist of lime.

Hog Snort

1 1/4 ounces coconut-flavored rum
3/4 ounce blue Curaçao
Splash sour mix
Pineapple juice

Add ice to a shaker. Pour the rum, blue Curaçao, and sour mix into the shaker. Fill the shaker with pineapple juice to measure 8 ounces. Shake and strain into an 8-ounce glass.

Goombay Smash

2 ounces coconut-flavored rum
Splash cream of coconut
1 ounce orange juice
Pineapple juice
1/4 ounce dark rum

Add ice to a shaker. Pour the coconut-flavored rum, cream of coconut, and orange juice into the shaker. Fill the shaker with pineapple juice to measure 8 ounces. Shake and strain into an 8-ounce glass. Float dark rum on top of the drink.

Margaritaville's Who's to Blame® Margarita

SERVES 4 TO 6

J immy Buffet arrived in Key West from Tennessee in 1971, escaping the cold weather and recovering from a divorce. He was introduced to Coconut Grove and then to Key West by his friends Jerry Jeff Walker (Mr. Bojangles) and Teressa "Murphy" Clark. The natural beauty of the island chain had a profound effect on him. What better place than this island outpost for Jimmy's friends to help him dispel his gloom?

He started his Margaritaville in Key West. He sat at a table one day and created his perfect margarita on a napkin. More margaritas followed. Here's one of the most popular drinks.

• •

2 tablespoons salt
1 lime wedge
1 1/2 ounces Margaritaville® Gold Tequila
　　(or tequila of your choice)
1/2 ounce triple sec (or other orange liqueur)
1/2 cup margarita mix

Place the salt on a plate. Wipe the rim of a margarita glass with a wedge of lime. Dip the rim into salt to form a ring of salt on the glass. Pour the tequila, triple sec, and margarita mix into a shaker. Shake well. Pour into the margarita glass.

Sloppy Joe's Bar Key West

There's a party 365 days a year at Sloppy Joe's Bar on Duval Street in Key West, but their New Year's Eve party is special. Duval Street is closed to traffic, and there's a band at their bar and an emcee on the roof of Sloppy Joe's. A giant, six-foot conch shell, created by artist Tobias McGregor, is dropped from the roof at midnight. Create your own Sloppy Joe party with these popular Sloppy Joe drinks.

EACH RECIPE SERVES 1

Sloppy Rita

This is their signature margarita, named after long-term employee Reta MacMakin-Root. She started as a bartender and is now a manager.

> 1 ounce tequila
> 1/2 ounce orange liqueur
> 5 ounces sour mix
> Splash orange juice
> 2 tablespoons salt
> 1 lime wedge
> 1 lime slice
> Dash club soda

Pour the tequila, orange liqueur, sour mix, and orange juice into a shaker of ice. Shake well. Place the salt on a plate. Wipe the lime wedge around the edge of a margarita glass. Dip the edge in the salt. Strain the contents of the shaker into the glass. Add a dash of club soda. Place the lime slice on the edge of the glass as a garnish.

Key West Lemonade

1 1/2 ounces lemon-flavored vodka
5 ounces sour mix
Splash of cranberry juice
Splash of lemon/lime-flavored soda
1 lemon slice

Fill a 12- to 14-ounce shaker with ice. Add the vodka, sour mix, cranberry juice, and lemon/lime soda. Shake well. Pour into a glass. Place the lemon slice on the edge of the glass as a garnish.

Papa Dobles

1 1/2 ounces light rum
4 ounces grapefruit juice
Splash of sour mix
Splash of grenadine
Squeeze of fresh lime
1 lime slice

Fill a 12- to 14-ounce shaker with ice. Add the rum, grapefruit juice, sour mix, grenadine, and lime juice. Shake well. Pour into a glass. Place the lime slice on the edge of the glass as a garnish.

Sloppy Sundowner

1 ounce dark rum
3 ounces orange juice
3 ounces pineapple juice
Drizzle of grenadine
1/2 ounce orange-flavored rum

Fill a 12- to 14-ounce shaker with ice. Add the dark rum, orange juice, pineapple juice, and grenadine. Shake well. Pour into a glass. Float orange-flavored rum on the top.

Lazy Days Key Lime Coolie

SERVES 1

Bartender Dave Ramia whipped up this drink in minutes, and it was a perfect start to what turned out to be a delicious evening.

With its position overlooking the ocean, its great food and large, friendly bar, Lazy Days is the perfect name for this Islamorada restaurant, which is a favorite among tourists and locals.

• •

2 ounces water
1/2 cup sugar
1/4 cup graham-cracker crumbs
1 1/2 ounces lemon-flavored vodka
1 ounce Licor 43
1/2 ounce key lime juice
1 small scoop vanilla ice cream

Place the water and sugar in a saucepan and cook over medium-low heat until the sugar dissolves and the liquid looks clear. Set aside to cool. Spoon the graham-cracker crumbs onto a plate. Dip the rim of a 14-ounce glass into the sugar solution and then into the graham-cracker crumbs to coat the rim of the glass. Measure 12 ounces of ice and pour into a blender. Add the vodka, Liqueur 43, key lime juice, and ice cream and blend. Pour into the prepared glass.

Key Lime Cosmopolitan

SERVES 1

The Marriott Beachside Hotel is tucked away on the east side of Key West away from the hustle and bustle of Duval Street. It is the island's only five-star resort. It's luxury with a laid-back atmosphere. The Tavern N Town restaurant invites you to relax and enjoy good food and great service with its casual elegance. It's fine to wear shorts.

They make a mean Key Lime Cosmopolitan. Bruno Leboucher, the restaurant director, gave me this recipe.

• •

    1 ounce key lime juice
    1/2 ounce cointreau
    1 1/2 ounces Grey Goose vodka
    1/2 ounce cranberry juice
    2 ounces simple syrup*
    1 thin lemon slice

Pour the key lime juice, cointreau, vodka, cranberry juice, and simple syrup into a shaker with ice. Shake and strain into a martini glass. Add a twist of lemon on the side of the glass as a garnish.

*Many tropical drinks call for simple syrup. It's made by mixing equal amounts of sugar and water together (1/4 cup water and 1/4 cup sugar). Dissolve the sugar in the water and then boil for 3 minutes. The liquid should remain clear. Cool and store in the refrigerator. It will keep for several weeks.

Key Lime Martini

SERVES 1

Looking out over the ocean just as the sun is setting is a special treat at the Upper Deck at Louie's Backyard. The top-floor tapas bar and outside deck are the perfect setting for the end of a Key West day. Nicole Garcia plied us with drinks, which made the setting even better. My favorite was her Key Lime Martini. With the rim of the martini glass coated in graham cracker crumbs, it was like drinking a key lime pie.

• •

2 tablespoons graham-cracker crumbs
Splash key lime juice plus juice for rim of martini glass
2 ounces vanilla vodka
Splash Licor 43
3 ounces sour or margarita mix

Place the graham cracker crumbs on a plate. Wipe a little key lime juice around the rim of a martini glass and dip the rim into the graham cracker crumbs. Add ice to a shaker or glass. Add the vodka, Licor 43, sour mix, and a splash of key lime juice. Shake and strain into the prepared martini glass.

Sundowners Key Largo

Sundowners restaurant in Key Largo is a perfect spot to sip a cocktail and watch the sunset. The views are spectacular day or night. My first visit was on a friend's boat. You can dock right at the restaurant. Sundowners started out as an open-air restaurant. It now has a covered restaurant with glass walls as well as an outdoor eating terrace. You can enjoy uninterrupted views of the bay from every seat.

EACH RECIPE SERVES 1

Hurricane 88

1 1/4 ounces passion fruit–flavored rum
3/4 ounce dark rum
2 ounces passion fruit nectar or juice
1 ounce orange juice
1 orange slice

Pour the ingredients, except the orange slice, into a shaker. Add ice and shake well. Pour into a hurricane-shaped* or cocktail glass. Garnish with the orange slice.

*Similar to an hourglass.

Hemingway Cocktail

1 1/4 ounces dark rum
1 1/4 ounces simple syrup *
3/4 ounce fresh lime juice

Pour the ingredients into a shaker with ice and shake vigorously. Pour into a small cocktail or martini-size glass.

*Many tropical drinks call for simple syrup. It's made by mixing equal amounts of sugar and water together (1/4 cup water and 1/4 cup sugar). Dissolve the sugar in the water and then boil for 3 minutes. The liquid should remain clear. Cool and store in the refrigerator. It will keep for several weeks.

The Fish House Spiegel Grove

SERVES 1

In 2002, the mothballed *USS Spiegel Grove* was towed to Key Largo and sunk in order to form an artificial reef. It actually sank and rolled over about six hours before its intended scuttling. The Fish House in Key Largo created this drink on the day it was scuttled.

• •

1/2 ounce coconut-flavored rum
1/2 ounce orange-flavored rum
1/2 ounce lemon-flavored rum
1 cup sour mix
Splash blue Curaçao

Place ice in a shaker and add the ingredients. Shake well and pour over ice in a 12-ounce glass.

To make a frozen drink, place 2 cups ice in a blender and add the drink ingredients. Blend until smooth. Pour into a 12-ounce glass.

Tiki Bar Magic

SERVES 1

The Holiday Isle Beach Resort and Marina is the home of the famous Tiki Bar where "Tiki" John (John Ebert) created the Rum Runner in the 1970s. It's become a sizeable resort area now, and the Tiki Bar is much larger. Bar manager Jakub Fusinski told me he created a drink called Magic, and it was.

• •

1 1/2 ounces raspberry vodka
8 ounces orange juice
3 ounces sour mix
Splash blue Curaçao

Add the raspberry vodka, orange juice, and sour mix to a shaker. Shake well. Half fill a 12-ounce glass with ice and pour in the mixture. Float the blue Curaçao on top.

Pirate's Painkiller

SERVES 1

Islamorada Fish Company sits facing west. It was originally owned by Dorothy and George Hertel, who ran a small fish market from this spot. Today it includes a fish market, the World Wide Sportsman, and the Zane Grey Lounge. The outdoor tiki hut on the beach serves this drink in a perfect spot to watch the sunset. With or without pain, it's a treat.

• •

1 1/4 ounces spiced rum
3 ounces cream of coconut
5 ounces pineapple juice
Sprinkle of ground nutmeg

Fill a shaker with ice. Add the rum, cream of coconut, and pineapple juice. Shake well. Half fill a 12-ounce glass with ice. Strain the drink from the shaker into the glass. Sprinkle nutmeg on top.

Breakfast

W ake up to a Keys breakfast. Nights are packed with fun, but even so, I found that Conchs arise to a hearty breakfast. I discovered a number of spots that take a delightfully creative approach to the morning meal. These sunny dishes will make welcome additions to your breakfast or brunch menus.

Is French toast your favorite? Bob's Bunz makes French toast from banana bread and serves it with fried bananas. Azur serves French toast sandwiched with a slice of creamy key lime pie and topped with a fresh berry compote. Both treat you to delicious variations on egg-dipped bread. Blue Heaven Pancakes filled with pecans and blueberries come out perfectly every time. Blue Crab Eggs Benedict is made with a freshly made crab cake, which is a perfect addition to this traditional egg dish with hollandaise sauce. Hawks Cay serves a European-style Birchermuesli, a light, creamy, and crunchy cereal that is packed with flavor. This section has a breakfast to fit every palate.

Alma's Birchermuesli

SERVES 4

Muesli was created by Dr. Bircher-Brenner near the end of the nineteeth century. Today there are many types of muesli. Chef Tony Glitz from Hawks Cay Resort on Duck Key created this muesli based on the original recipe from the Swiss doctor.

Fresh and dried fruit and nuts are combined with rolled oats, honey, and soy milk to make this flavorful cereal. Make it the night before and it will be ready for your breakfast the next day.

• •

2 cups rolled oats
1/4 cup sliced almonds
2 tablespoons dried cherries
2 tablespoons raisins
2 tablespoons walnut pieces
2 tablespoons macadamia nuts
2 tablespoons pecans
4 tablespoons honey
10 ounces soy milk
1 cup shredded green apple
1/2 cup half-and-half

Mix the oats, almonds, cherries, raisins, walnuts, macadamia nuts, pecans, honey, soy milk, and apple together. Refrigerate overnight. If thick, add half-and-half to loosen. Divide among 4 bowls and serve.

Blue Heaven Pancakes

SERVES 4

This old nineteenth-century Key West clapboard house was once a bordello, and in the 1930s, Ernest Hemingway refereed cock fighting matches there. Today you can still peek through the sliding peepholes into the tiny rooms from the Bordello Gallery above the restaurant. This was all long before Richard and Suanne Hatch turned Blue Heaven into one of Key West's most popular restaurants. The sign on the door reads: "Blue Heaven, serving heaven on a fork and sin in a glass."

When I went there one Sunday morning, the restaurant was packed and the diners in the courtyard shared space with some of the roosters and chickens that roam freely around Key West.

Richard Hatch says that these pancakes are one of their most popular morning dishes.

• •

2 cups flour
1 tablespoon baking soda
1 teaspoon salt
1/4 cup sugar
2 eggs
2 to 4 tablespoons beer
1 1/3 cups milk
Splash cider vinegar
8 teaspoons canola oil, divided use
2 cups blueberries or thinly sliced bananas
1/2 cup broken pecans
Best-quality maple syrup

Place the flour, baking soda, salt, and sugar in a bowl. Make a hole in the center of the mixture and add the eggs, beer, milk, and cider vinegar. Stir the liquid to gradually incorporate the dry ingredients. Add 4 teaspoons oil and stir. Heat a heavy skillet over medium-high heat. Add the remaining 4 teaspoons oil to the skillet. Add the blueberries or bananas and pecans to the mix just before cooking the pancakes. Spoon 1/4 cup batter into the skillet. When bubbles start to form, turn the pancake over and cook for 30 seconds to a minute. Continue to make more pancakes using the same method. Serve pancakes and pass the maple syrup. Makes 12 small pancakes.

Blue Crab Eggs Benedict

SERVES 4

People line up for breakfast and lunch at the Islamorada Bakery and Bob's Bunz, where the baked goods are the show. Owner Gloria Teague, a scuba diver, made her way to the Keys and opened a scuba diving shop. She met a pastry chef, Robert (Bob) Spencer, Jr., and decided to team up with him to open their bakery. Her organizational skills and his amazing baked goods have made this an Islamorada favorite. He makes over 350 wedding cakes and 700 birthday cakes a year.

The restaurant features a full range of eggs, waffles, cereals, and fruit. One of their most popular breakfasts is their Blue Crab Eggs Benedict. The base is an English muffin, topped with a blue crab cake, a poached egg, and hollandaise sauce.

• •

Crab Cakes

1/2 pound blue crab meat
1 egg
1/2 cup bread crumbs
1/2 cup diced celery
2 tablespoons diced onion
2 tablespoons mayonnaise
1 teaspoon mustard
1 tablespoon lemon juice
1 teaspoon Worcestershire sauce
1/4 teaspoon hot pepper sauce
1 teaspoon Old Bay seasoning
1/2 teaspoon salt
1 tablespoon butter

Place all the ingredients, except the butter, in a bowl and mix well. Shape into 8 crab cakes about 3 inches in diameter. Each one should fit nicely on an English muffin. Heat the butter in a large skillet over medium-high heat. Add the crab cakes and sauté for 2 minutes. Turn and sauté for 2 minutes. Remove from heat.

Hollandaise Sauce

2 egg yolks
1/4 cup water
1 tablespoon lemon juice
6 tablespoons cold butter
Salt and freshly ground pepper to taste

Add the egg yolks, water, and lemon juice to a saucepan. Whisk until blended. Place over medium heat. Stir with a whisk until bubbles appear around the edges. Stir in the butter, one tablespoon at a time, making sure the butter is melted before adding the next tablespoon. Whisk the mixture until it starts to thicken. If the sauce starts to break down or curdle, add 1 or 2 tablespoons boiling water to stabilize it. Season with salt and pepper.

Linda's Quick Hollandaise Sauce

I make a quick hollandaise sauce in the blender. It takes only seconds and is almost always successful.

Mix the water and egg yolks in a blender. Melt the butter until it is foaming but not burning. With the motor running, very slowly pour the butter into the blender. Watch the mixture to be sure it is thickening. Stop pouring and let the machine run for a few seconds if it looks too thin. Add the lemon juice and continue to blend. Spoon immediately over the eggs.

The sauce should be made at the last minute. If made an hour ahead, gently rewarm it over warm water, whisking constantly. Be careful, as it may break down or curdle.

Eggs Benedict

4 English muffins
8 large eggs

Split the English muffins in half and toast. Place a top and bottom on each of 4 plates. Place one crab cake on each muffin half. Heat 2 to 3 inches of water to a simmer in a large saucepan or deep skillet. Break the eggs into a saucer one at a time. Slip the eggs into the water. Poach until the whites are set and the yolks are just beginning to thicken. Place one egg on each crab cake. Spoon hollandaise over the top and serve.

Tropical Coffee Cake

SERVES 10 TO 12

Hidden from the Overseas Highway in Key Largo, the Key Largo Conch House looks like a Victorian home. I asked the owner, Laura Dreaver, about it and she said it was built in 1994 to look like a Victorian Bahamas home. Their porch is a perfect setting to enjoy a Keys breakfast. Their Tropical Coffee Cake is made in-house fresh every day.

• •

Vegetable oil spray
3 cups flour
3 teaspoons baking powder
1 teaspoon salt
2 cups sugar
1 cup key lime juice
1/2 cup pineapple juice
1 cup butter
3 eggs
1 small box vanilla instant pudding
1/2 cup crushed pineapple
1/2 cup macadamia nuts, chopped
1 cup shredded coconut
1/2 cup sugar

Preheat the oven to 350°F Grease a 9x13-inch pan with vegetable oil spray. Mix the flour, baking powder, salt, 2 cups sugar, key lime juice, pineapple juice, butter, eggs, and vanilla pudding together until blended. Add the pineapple and mix well. Mix the macadamia nuts, coconut, and 1/2 cup sugar together in a separate bowl.

Pour half of the batter into the greased pan. Sprinkle half of the nut mixture over the batter and pour the remaining batter into the pan. Sprinkle the remaining nut mixture over the top. Bake for 55 to 60 minutes.

Banana Bread French Toast with Fried Bananas

SERVES 4

After tasting this scrumptious breakfast dish at the Islamorada Bakery and Bob's Bunz, I couldn't wait to have the recipe. Baker Bob Spencer gave me the secret to his Banana Bread French Toast: It's his recipe for the banana bread (p. 243).

Make Bob's banana bread or use a good-quality store-bought banana bread. Bob serves his French toast with Fried Bananas.

• •

6 eggs
1/2 cup heavy cream
1/2 cup milk
1 tablespoon vanilla extract
1/2 teaspoon cinnamon
1/4 teaspoon nutmeg
2 tablespoons brown sugar
8 slices Bob's Bunz Banana Bread (see p. 243)
3 tablespoons butter

Mix the eggs, heavy cream, milk, vanilla extract, cinnamon, nutmeg, and brown sugar together in a large bowl. Add 2 slices banana bread at a time to the bowl and turn to make sure both sides are in the mixture. Remove and continue until all the slices have absorbed the mixture.

Heat the butter in a griddle or large skillet over medium-high heat and add the bread in 1 layer. Cook for 3 minutes or until the bread is golden and turn. Cook for 3 minutes. If using a large skillet instead of a griddle, cook the bread in batches. Divide the pieces among 4 plates and serve with Fried Bananas.

Fried Bananas

4 ripe medium-size bananas
1 cup panko (Japanese-style bread crumbs)
Canola oil for frying

Peel the bananas and cut into thirds. Roll them in the bread crumbs, making sure all sides are coated. Heat the oil in a deep fryer to 350°F. Add the bananas and fry for 1 minute or until golden. Drain on paper towels. Serve with French Toast.

Key Lime Pie French Toast with Berry Compote

SERVES 4

Tucked into a quiet corner several blocks from Duval Street in Old Town, Key West, the Azur restaurant is a local gem. Sitting on their shaded terrace, I watched the locals walk by and talked with Chef Drew Wenzel. Drew migrated from the Southern United States to Germany in 1994 and opened Grace Land, a restaurant featuring Southern American cuisine. He delightedly told me that he used recipes from my book, *Keys Cuisine*, very successfully at the restaurant in Germany. He sold Grace Land in 2003, and on a rainy, cold day in Germany, a friend in Key West called and asked for his help. He came to Key West for two months and the owners wouldn't let him go. He fell in love with the sunshine and, along with college buddy Michael Mosi, opened Azur.

He told me his Key Lime Pie French Toast is a signature dish. He serves it with a Berry Compote.

Make the key lime pie a day ahead. It cuts into squares better when it is cooled. This will be a flat pie about 1 to 1 1/2 inches thick. Drew calls for Texas bread. This is a very light, white, thick-cut bread. It can be found in most supermarkets. Any light, airy bread can be used. The compote can be made a day ahead.

• •

Pie Crust

2 cups graham-cracker crumbs
1/2 cup brown sugar
1 cup butter, melted

Preheat the oven to 250°F. Mix the graham cracker crumbs, brown sugar, and melted butter together in a 9x13x2-inch baking pan. Pat the crumbs to form a crust in the bottom of the pan. Bake for 20 min. Cool.

Pie Filling

4 egg yolks
1 14-ounce can sweetened condensed milk
1/2 cup key lime juice

Preheat the oven to 325°F. Mix the egg yolks, condensed milk, and key lime juice together in a large mixing bowl until combined. Pour on top of the cooled pie crust and bake until firm, about 25 minutes or until firm but not brown.

Berry Compote

2 cups frozen mixed berries, divided in half
1 cup apple juice
1/4 cup sugar
1/2 lemon, squeezed and strained
1/2 orange, squeezed and strained
1 tablespoon cornstarch
2 tablespoons water

Combine the apple juice, sugar, lemon juice, and orange juice in a saucepan. Add half the frozen berries and heat over high heat until the liquid boils. Mix together the cornstarch and water and add to the berries. Stir until the berries thicken. Remove from the heat and add the remaining frozen berries. Do not heat further. This helps the remaining berries keep their shape and structure. Set aside.

French Toast

8 slices Texas toast
6 whole eggs
4 tablespoons cream
1/2 teaspoon cinnamon
4 tablespoons butter
Confectioners' sugar for serving

Mix the eggs, cream, and cinnamon together. Place the bread in the egg mixture, turning the bread to make sure both sides absorb the liquid. Melt the butter in a skillet over medium heat. Sauté the bread slices for 1 minute. Turn and cook the second side for one minute.

Cut the key lime pie into 8 squares about the same size as the bread. Then cut the squares in half from one corner to the opposite corner, making 2 triangles. Cut the French toast in the same fashion.

Lay one triangle of toast, point side up, on a platter. Place a key lime pie triangle on the toast and continue to alternate the toast and key lime pie on the platter. Spoon compote over the top and sprinkle with confectioners' sugar. Bring the platter to the table and serve family style. Or, layer the toast and pie on 4 individual plates.

La Super Crepe

SERVES 1

Hungry for their famous crepes, I wandered down Duval Street for an amazing breakfast at Banana Café. Danilo Castillo was standing at the large crepe wheel making the crepes to order. He told me that La Super, a crepe filled with egg, ham, cheese, sausage, and topped with a mushroom sauce, is his specialty. I ordered La Super and watched him make it. The thin, filled crepe was light as a feather and melted in my mouth.

• •

1/4 cup flour
1/2 teaspoon salt
1 egg
1/4 cup milk
2 tablespoons canola, divided use
1 egg
1/4 cup shredded Gruyère cheese
1 slice honey roasted ham
1 4-inch cooked breakfast sausage

Sift the flour and salt into a bowl. In a second bowl, mix the egg, milk, and 1 tablespoon oil together. Make a well in the flour and add the egg mixture. Mix the flour into the egg mixture. Stir gently until smooth. Let stand while preparing the remaining ingredients. (This amount will make 2 10-inch crepes.)

Heat the remaining 1 tablespoon oil in a large 10-inch skillet or crepe pan over medium-high heat until it starts to smoke. Add about 1/2 soup ladle of the batter to the pan and roll the pan to spread the batter evenly. Crack the egg onto the batter and spread it over the crepe. Sprinkle the cheese over the egg. Place the ham slice in the middle of the crepe and place the sausage in the middle of the ham. When bubbles start to show on the crepe, fold one edge to the middle and fold the other edge to meet it. Fold the ends to the center to make a package. Place on a plate and spoon mushroom sauce over the crepe. Serves one. Double the filling and mushroom sauce to fill 2 crepes.

Mushroom Sauce

1/2 tablespoon butter
1/2 cup sliced mushrooms
1/4 cup heavy cream
1/4 cup chicken broth
Salt and freshly ground black pepper to taste

Melt the butter in a saucepan over medium heat and add the mushrooms. Sauté until the mushrooms soften, about 5 minutes. Add the cream and broth. Bring to a simmer and reduce slightly. Add salt and pepper to taste. Set aside.

Soups

Soups are an inviting start to any meal. Many are a meal in themselves. It is natural that there is an abundance of fish soups and chowders. Conch chowder is served in most restaurants. MA's Fish Camp Restaurant's Bahamian Conch Chowder is spicy, hot, and filled with conch and vegetables.

The secret to a good fish soup is the quality of the fish. If you can't find the fish called for in these recipes, then use the best and freshest available to you; stay away from dark-fleshed oily fish such as mackerel or salmon when making soup.

If you're looking for an intriguing soup, try Hawks Cay's Sweet Potato Bisque. Coconut and ginger add unusual flavors to the sweet potatoes.

Cold soups on hot nights are as refreshing as hot soups are satisfying on cold nights. Hawks Cay's Mango and Crab Gazpacho, with its bright crisp flavor, adds a tropical twist to this dish of Spanish origin.

Enjoy a light Keys supper by adding some good, crusty bread and cold beer or a cool glass of Chablis.

Fish Stock

MAKES ABOUT 2 QUARTS

Fish stock is the base of many soups and sauces. Here's a simple and unusual one given to me by Charlotte Miller, chef at Hawks Cay Resort and Marina's Tom's Harbor House restaurant on Duck Key. This casual restaurant sits right on the marina and has access to great seafood fresh off the docks. Chef Charlotte knows the local fishing captains and keeps in daily contact with them as they come back from their day of fishing. Whenever she has a free moment, she hops on their boats and is well known for being a competitive angler.

Charlotte makes her stock using ice cubes instead of water. The ice keeps the stock cleaner. It doesn't get cloudy. She likes to use the carcass from mutton snappers. Their large fins have more gelatin.

- -

1 tablespoon canola oil
1 leek, cleaned and sliced
1 small onion, sliced
2 ribs celery, sliced
1 whole carcass snapper or other non-oily fish
Ice cubes to cover fish
1 bay leaf
Several parsley stalks

Heat the oil in a large saucepan over medium-high heat. Add the leek, onion, and celery. Sauté for 2 minutes without coloring the vegetables. Add the fish carcass and cover it with ice cubes. Add the bay leaf and parsley stalks. Cover with a lid and cook over low heat for 2 hours. It's ready when the tail webbing disappears.

Alma's Yellow Tomato, Mango, and Crab Gazpacho

SERVES 4

Bright and crisp, this is a Keys take on traditional gazpacho. It tastes great on its own or swirl the avocado cream into the soup just before it's served. Chef Tony Glitz from Alma Restaurant at Hawks Cay Resort on Duck Key created this recipe. Chef Tony serves this gazpacho in martini glasses. Use any type of attractive glass or soup bowl.

2 yellow tomatoes, cut into wedges
1/2 cup mango cubes
2 tablespoons sherry vinegar (or rice vinegar)
1/4 cup cilantro leaves
1/2 small shallot, skin removed
1 tablespoon sugar
Pinch salt
2 tablespoons olive oil
1 cup lump crabmeat, flaked

Place the tomatoes, mango, vinegar, cilantro, shallot, sugar, and salt in a blender. Blend until smooth, stopping to push the ingredients down from the sides of the blender, if needed. Remove to a bowl and stir in the olive oil. Pour into 4 martini glasses. Swirl in the avocado cream. Place 1/4 cup crabmeat in the center of each glass.

Avocado Cream

1 ripe small avocado, seed and skin removed
3/4 cup chopped cilantro
1/2 cup heavy cream
2 tablespoons lime juice

Cut the avocado into wedges and place in a food processor. Add the cilantro, cream, and lime juice. Blend until smooth.

Sweet Potato Bisque

SERVES 4

East meets West with this light bisque. Coconut milk and ginger give sweet potatoes an Asian flavor. Chef Charlotte Miller from Tom's Harbor House at Hawks Cay Resort on Duck Key grew up in an international house at the university where her parents worked, and there she learned to use many types of ethnic flavors. She created this soup for vegetarian guests at Tom's Harbor House.

• •

2 pounds sweet potatoes
1 cup canned unsweetened coconut milk
3 cups water
1 2-inch piece ginger, peeled
6 tablespoons chopped shallots (about 3 large shallots)
3 garlic cloves, crushed
1/2 cup shredded coconut
Zest of 2 limes

Preheat the oven or toaster oven to 350°F. Peel the potatoes and cut them into 1-inch cubes. Place in a large saucepan and add the coconut milk and water. Cover with a lid and simmer for 15 minutes over medium-high heat. The potatoes should be soft. Place in a blender with the ginger, shallots, and garlic and blend until smooth.

While the potatoes cook, place the coconut in one layer on a baking tray and toast in the oven until golden, about 10 minutes. Watch to make sure they don't burn.

Pour soup into 4 soup bowls and sprinkle the coconut and lime zest on top.

Santiago's Shrimp Bisque

SERVES 4

Off the beaten path in the Bahamian Village section of Key West is a small tapas restaurant, Santiago's Bodega, run by owners Jason Dugan and Angelo Blecher. It quickly became a local favorite when it opened, but word of mouth travels. Jimmy Buffet often dines there, and other stars find their way to this charming spot now, too.

● ●

2 tablespoons butter
1 cup diced white onion
3 cups clam juice
1 tablespoon long-grain white rice
3/4 pound cooked shrimp
3 tablespoons tomato paste
1 teaspoon cayenne pepper
1/2 cup half-and-half
1/2 cup heavy cream
Salt and pepper to taste

Melt the butter in a large saucepan over medium-high heat. Add the onions and slowly cook until they are transparent but not colored. Add the clam juice and bring to a boil. Add the rice and half cover with a lid. Cook until the rice is tender, about 8 minutes. Turn off the heat and add the shrimp. Let cool for 10 minutes. Puree with an immersion blender or in a blender until smooth. Return to the heat and add the tomato paste, cayenne pepper, half-and-half, cream, and salt and pepper to taste. Bring to a simmer for a few minutes, stirring constantly. Serve immediately or chill and store in the refrigerator.

MA's Bahamian Conch Chowder

SERVES 4

Mike Burgeen and Andy Putetti, who put the *MA* in MA's Fish Camp restaurant in Islamorada, are professional sportfishing guides who decided to open a restaurant. Now they fish and cook. Mike and Andy's Bahamian Chowder is a specialty there.

They infuse the chowder with habanero peppers. According to Andy, "They make hot taste sweet." These are one of the hottest peppers known. He recommends removing the peppers after the vegetables are sautéed.

• •

1/2 pound conch
1 tablespoon butter
3/4 cup sliced onion
3/4 cup sliced carrots
3/4 cup sliced celery
1/2 habanero pepper, seeds and ribs removed
     (other hot peppers can be substituted)
4 cups fish broth
1/2 cup tomato paste
2 teaspoons dried thyme
3 teaspoons Old Bay seasoning
2 cups russet potatoes, peeled and cut into 1-inch cubes
Salt and freshly ground black pepper to taste

Remove the orange foot from the conch and chop in a food processor. Heat the butter in a large saucepan over medium-high heat and add the onions, carrots, celery, and habanero pepper. Sauté until the vegetables begin to shrivel, about 5 minutes. Remove the habanero pepper. Add the fish broth and tomato paste. Stir to combine the paste with the broth. Add the thyme and Old Bay seasoning. Add the potatoes and conch, bring to a simmer, cover, and cook for 25 minutes. Add salt and pepper to taste.

Turtle Chowder

SERVES 4

When the Green Turtle Inn opened in 1947, green turtle was a staple food in the Keys. With a lack of refrigeration and fresh meat, people lived on what they could catch. Green turtles, weighing in at 250 to 300 pounds, are high in protein and good to eat. The United States banned the use of green turtle meat in 1978 in order to protect the diminishing species. Other species of turtle meat are available. This soup works well with boneless, skinless chicken breast or lobster.

• •

2 tablespoons butter
1 tablespoon flour
1/2 pound turtle meat (or boneless, skinless chicken
      breast or lobster), cut into 1/2-inch dice
1/4 teaspoon dried oregano
1/4 tablespoon blackened seasoning
Several drops hot pepper sauce
1/4 tablespoon canola oil
1/4 cup diced carrots
1/4 cup diced onion
1/4 cup diced celery
2 garlic cloves, crushed
2 tablespoons dry sherry
3 ounces canned diced tomatoes
1 tablespoon Worcestershire sauce
8 cups chicken stock
1 pound russet potatoes, cut into 1/2-inch cubes
Dash cayenne pepper
Salt and freshly ground black pepper to taste

Melt the butter in a small saucepan over medium heat. Add the flour and mix thoroughly to make a roux. Set aside.

Place the turtle in a bowl and add the oregano, blackened seasoning, and hot pepper sauce. Toss well. Heat the oil in a large saucepan over medium-high heat, add the turtle, and brown on all sides, about 2 minutes. Add the carrots, onion, celery, and garlic. Sauté until the vegetables are soft. Add the roux to the saucepan and mix well. Add the sherry and reduce slightly. Add the diced tomatoes, Worcestershire sauce, chicken stock, potatoes, and cayenne pepper. Bring to a boil, reduce the heat, and simmer gently for 30 minutes. Add salt and pepper to taste.

Seafood Cioppino

SERVES 4

Cioppino is an Italian fish stew that is traditionally made with whatever fish was freshly caught that day. John Malocsay at Bentley's Rawbar and Restaurant in Islamorada makes his cioppino with a marinara sauce spiced with garlic and sherry. You can use any combination of fish and shellfish; just make sure it's all very fresh.

• •

8 clams
8 mussels
4 tablespoons butter
3 garlic cloves, crushed
8 scallops
1/2 pound mahimahi or other fish fillet,
    cut into bite-size pieces
8 peeled shrimp
1 Florida lobster tail, cut into 4 pieces
1 cup fish stock
3/4 cup marinara sauce
2 tablespoons dry sherry
1 cup snow crab or other crab as garnish

If any of the clams or mussels are open, tap them on the counter to close and discard any that don't close. Wash the clams and mussels under cold running water. Heat the butter in a large saucepan over medium-high heat. Add the garlic, scallops, mahimahi, and shrimp. Sauté for 2 minutes and then divide among 4 large soup bowls. Add the clams, mussels, and lobster to the saucepan. Add the fish stock, marinara sauce, and sherry. Cover the saucepan with a lid and bring to a simmer. Cook for 3 minutes or until the clams and mussels open. Discard any that do not open. Spoon the soup and shellfish over the fish in the soup bowls and sprinkle the crab on top.

Main Courses

Seafood

The Florida Keys have some of the best fish and shellfish in the world. Many varieties are staples on the menus, including a few Keys specialties: conch, stone crabs, Keys pink shrimp, and Florida lobster. Many chefs in the Keys, who have worked in restaurants around the world, commented to me on the extraordinary flavor, freshness, and texture of the fish. Their dishes are wonderful because the fish is so fresh. When making these recipes, be sure to buy the very freshest fish available and substitute it in the recipes.

The Florida Keys also provide one of the best sportfishing areas of the world, and the local chefs take advantage by serving some of the more unusual fish species, such as tilefish and cobia. Hawks Cay Resort and Marina on Duck Key is home to many of the charter boats that fish in this famous area. Sportfishermen flock to the Keys to enjoy game fishing. The captains like to cook the fish they catch, too, and they've shared their special recipes here.

Knowing how to cook fish is as important as knowing how to buy it. The section entitled "Hints on Cooking Fish" will help you prepare these and your own fish recipes.

You'll find a recipe here to suit any mood, whether it's fish on the grill, sautéed with a Key Lime Butter Sauce, or broiled with spicy salsa. Everything you need to enjoy the bounty of the seas is here.

Meat and Poultry

Landlubbers are not left out in the Keys. Meat and poultry are served in a variety of Keys recipes. Charlotte Miller at Hawks Cay Resort braises her pork in sangria and uses it to make delicious sliders or serves it with polenta. Michael's Stuffed Veal Chops is a special treat, and Mrs. Mac's Kitchen's Churrasco Steak with Tijuana Sauce keeps her customers coming back for more. Jennifer Cornell created Sesame Almond Chicken with Mango Banana Chutney by incorporating local flavors. And then there's jerk chicken that has drifted from Jamaica to the Keys, with its delicious, sweet, and spicy blend of herbs.

Types of Shellfish and Fish

Florida Lobster

Florida lobster is also called spiny lobster or spiny crawfish. This shellfish is easily recognized by the prominent spines on its body and five pairs of legs. Unlike the Maine lobster, it does not have claws. The body is discarded and the large, meaty tail can be boiled, broiled, steamed, deep-fried, or grilled. Lobster season is controlled and runs from August 6 through March 31. Frozen Florida lobster tails are sold all over the United States and will work well in these recipes.

Stone Crabs

Stone crabs, with their large red and black claws, are a Florida institution. Only the claws are taken from the crabs when they are caught. The bodies are thrown back into the water, where they will grow a new claw within about eighteen months. The claws are cooked either on the fishing boats or as soon as they are brought in from the boats. Fresh stone crab claws cooked to order are best, but this luxury is available only to those who catch them or know someone who does. The claws cannot be reheated. They take on an ammonia taste if they are.

In an interview with me on my South Florida National Public Radio program, Joanne Bass, granddaughter of Joe Weiss, the original owner of the famous Joe's Stone Crab restaurant on South Beach, related her story of how stone crabs became a Florida treasure. A Harvard professor came to Joe with a bag of live stone crabs and asked if they could be boiled or what he could do with them. Joe decided to throw them in a pot of water and boil them. They were a hit. Later, he developed a method of cooking and chilling the claws. They're now served throughout the United States and beyond.

Blue Crabs

Blue crab fishing is popular in the Upper Keys, and many crabs are caught right along Card Sound Road in Key Largo. They can be found in salt and fresh water from Cape Cod to Florida and in abundance in the bays and estuaries of the Gulf of Mexico and Chesapeake Bay. You can buy jumbo lump crabmeat in a can or frozen for the recipes here.

Key West Pink Shrimp

"Pink gold" is what the natives of the Keys call these shrimp. They're big, juicy Key West pink shrimp. When I first saw them, I asked the girl behind the fish counter why the raw shrimp were pink. The surprised girl said, "I've never seen them any other color." Fresh shrimp play a large role in Keys cooking. Shrimping became an important industry in the Keys in the 1970s. If you don't have pink shrimp, these recipes will work very well with any type of shrimp.

Conch

Conch (pronounced "konk") is a spiral-shaped gastropod. It lives in a large spiral shell and can be very tough. It needs to be tenderized before use. It can also be eaten raw. One Keys friend tells me that he used to go out fishing with his grandparents and take along all the fixings for a conch salad. They would catch the conch and eat it right there on the boat. Today, because they have been overfished, it is illegal to fish for conch off the United States coast. As a result, we now get our conch imported and frozen. Those of you on the West Coast will find that the recipes work well with abalone substituted for conch.

Tenderizing Conch

There are several schools of thought on whether conch should be tenderized or not. I have eaten raw or marinated conch and it was beautifully tender. I have also eaten cooked conch and couldn't chew it at all. Much depends on the quality and freshness of the conch. The color of the meat should be white with pink and orange edges. It should not smell fishy. To be on the safe side, ask for the conch to be tenderized when you buy it. There is a machine that does the job in seconds. If tenderizing at home, first cut off the orange fin and foot. Trim off any dark pieces of skin. Then slice the conch in half lengthwise to make it thinner. Place the meat between two pieces of plastic wrap. Using a meat mallet or the bottom of a bottle, pound diagonally in one direction and then again in the opposite direction.

Conch, Nickname for Natives

Conch is a term used to describe the British who lived in Key West during the time of the Revolutionary War and didn't want to fight against England. During the War, they fled to English colonies such as the Grand Bahamas and then drifted back to Key West in the 1830s. They were seafarers and conch was their staple food. The shell was used as a horn and as a symbol on their clan standards. Today, natives of long standing adopt the name, but this angers the descendants of the so-called real Conchs. One legend holds that in the days of the buccaneers, unknown ships would hoist a friendly conch shell to the foremast to gain entry to a port. More often than not, they would enter the harbor, raise the Jolly Roger, and sack the settlement.

The Conch Republic

On April 18, 1982, the United States border patrol set up a roadblock in Florida to prohibit illegal aliens from entering the country. The Keys were treated as a foreign land, and people entering or leaving had to prove United States citizenship. On April 23, 1982, in mock protest, Key West declared its independence from the United States and called itself the Conch Republic.

Grouper

Grouper is the generic name for 162 known fish species. They are members of the same family as sea bass. White-fleshed and firm, they keep their shape and moisture when cooked. Some of the species have become overfished and can only be caught at certain times of the year.

Snapper

There are about 150 species of snapper. Hogfish, yellowtail, and mutton are very popular in the Keys. Their delicate flesh doesn't keep well, even when placed on ice, so the fresher the better. Their fillets are so sweet they don't need much cooking. The hogfish is a special Keys delicacy. The head actually resembles a pig's snout, and they are said to grunt in the water.

Dolphin/Mahimahi

Dolphin is a light, white fish and, due to its name, is often confused with the mammal of the same name. So, it is now often called by its Hawaiian name, mahimahi. On my first trip to the Keys, I was introduced to this delicious, flaky fish by my next-door neighbor. Every day around five, his boat would return to his dock and he would start to clean his catch. When the pelicans began to congregate, waiting for leftover tidbits, I knew he was back. One day I finally asked him what type of fish he caught. On many evenings after that, I found a beautifully cleaned fillet of dolphin on my doorstep.

Tuna

Tuna are members of the mackerel family, but their taste is very different. In fact, even among the many species of tuna, the taste can vary considerably. Yellowfin tuna is also called by its Hawaiian name, ahi tuna, and is used widely in raw tuna dishes. Blackfin tuna is the smallest tuna species. Both are delicately flavored and worth searching out; they work well with the recipes here. Yellowfin and blackfin tuna can be found in local markets in the Keys and bought from local fishermen at the end of their fishing day. The dark-meat bonito tuna is strong tasting and I prefer not to use it. Be sure to use tuna that is as fresh as possible. If serving raw tuna, ask for yellowfin sushi-grade tuna.

Cobia

Cobia is a large fish, weighing from thirty to fifty pounds. It is often mistaken for shark, as it is found near the surface and close to shore. Cobia is a game fish and very good to eat. The meat is firm and white. It is a good fish to smoke. Cobia is served in the Keys when local fishermen show up at restaurants to sell their catch of the day.

Hints on Cooking Fish

One secret to enjoying great fish is to buy the freshest fish possible. The other secret is knowing how to cook it. Overcooked fish can be dry and tasteless. Here are some hints on cooking fish successfully.

Grilling

Grilling fresh fish brings out its natural flavor. The beautiful Keys weather is perfect for grilling year-round. You can light up the grill and cook outside and watch the sunset. However, grilling has become a year-round sport for everyone, even in the snow. So here are some tips.

Make sure your grill grates are clean. Preheat the grill about 5 minutes before cooking. Oil the fish and sprinkle with salt and pepper to taste. To tell whether the fish is cooked, press it with a finger. The fish should break into firm flakes.

Whole fish or firm-textured fish such as swordfish or tuna steaks is best for grilling. Fragile fish or thin fillets can fall apart and are difficult to move or turn on the grill. It's best to leave the skin on and start with the skin side down. Using a grill rack or grill topper is helpful, since it can be moved around on the grill and helps prevent the fish from sticking to the grill grates. If a whole fish is very thick, make a couple of diagonal slashes across the body on both sides so the heat will penetrate better.

Fillet Grilling Chart

1/2-inch fillet, over direct heat: 2 minutes per side
3/4-inch fillet, over direct heat: 2 to 3 minutes per side
1-inch fillet, over direct heat: 4 to 5 minutes per side

Avoid overcooking whole fish and steaks by placing the fish in the center of the grill, over direct heat, and searing them. Turn to sear the second side and then move the fish to the edge or to indirect heat. A general rule of thumb is to cook fish for ten minutes for each inch of thickness, measured in the thickest part of the fish. Remember that the fish will continue to cook in its own heat for a few minutes after it is removed from the grill.

Poaching

Poaching means to cook fish in a liquid, usually a white wine and water bath, in order to help preserve its moisture. This is an excellent method of cooking fish that will be served cold or at room temperature. The liquid should just cover the fish and be brought only to a simmer. Do not let the liquid boil; it will make the fish rubbery. If you are going to serve the fish cold or at room temperature, then undercook it and remove the pan from the heat. Let the fish cool in the liquid and it will remain juicy and tender.

Broiling

Be sure to preheat the broiler. I put a baking sheet or pan in to preheat as well. This way the radiant heat from the pan will cook the fish on the bottom and it will not need turning. Broil about 4 to 5 inches from the heat.

Frying

Frying is very popular in the Keys. It seals in the juices and creates a tasty outer coating. It's important to use fresh, clean frying oil. I prefer to fry fish at between 350°F and 375°F. If the oil is not hot enough, the fish will absorb it and become heavy. If the oil is too hot, the outer coating will burn and the inside won't be done. Fry just a few pieces at a time so they won't stick together, and you'll be able to control the cooking. Serve fried fish immediately. If left to sit, the trapped steam that is keeping the fish moist will escape, making the crust soggy. A piece of fish that is 1 to 2 inches thick will fry in 2 to 3 minutes. Larger pieces will take only a few minutes longer.

Sautéing

This method is best for fillets or flatfish. Make sure you use a heavy-bottomed pan so that the heat is evenly distributed. Melt the butter or oil so that it covers the bottom of the pan, and do not use a lid. Sauté the fish until it is a golden color on both sides.

Green Curried Keys Shrimp, Steamed Coconut Rice, Stir-Fried Broccoli Slaw

SERVES 4

hef Charlotte Miller from Tom's Harbor House at Hawks Cay Resort on Duck Key mentioned that she grew up in an international house on the college campus where her parents worked. She learned about many exciting ethnic flavors there. For this dish, she makes her own Thai green curry sauce and combines it with sweet Keys pink shrimp. She says you can also buy green curry sauce, found in the ethnic section of many markets, to make this dish. She serves the dish over Steamed Rice with a sweet coconut flavor and with Stir-Fried Broccoli Slaw.

Green curry paste is also available in markets. If using the paste, mix 1 tablespoon paste with 4 ounces canned unsweetened coconut milk.

• •

For sauce:
1 stalk lemongrass, white part only
1/2 bunch cilantro, stems removed
1/2 bunch fresh mint, stems removed
3 garlic cloves, crushed
1 1/2-inch piece fresh ginger, peeled
1 jalapeño pepper, seeded
4 ounces unsweetened coconut milk
Or:
1 cup bottled green curry sauce

Blend the lemon grass, cilantro, mint, garlic, ginger, and jalapeño pepper together in a food processor. Add the coconut milk and blend to a smooth sauce.

For shrimp:
2 tablespoons canola oil
1 1/2 pounds peeled shrimp

Heat the oil in a large skillet over medium-high heat and add the shrimp. Toss for 1 minute. Add the sauce and stir for 2 minutes or until the shrimp turn red.

Steamed Coconut Rice

1 cup canned unsweetened coconut milk
1 cup water
1 cup basmati rice
Salt and freshly ground black pepper to taste
2 scallions, sliced

Bring the coconut milk and water to a boil in a large saucepan over high heat. Add the rice and boil for 5 minutes. Cover with a lid, and turn the heat down to very low. Steam for 20 minutes. Do not open the lid during this time. Fluff the rice and add salt and pepper to taste. Sprinkle the scallions on top.

Stir-Fried Broccoli Slaw

2 tablespoons canola oil
2 garlic cloves, crushed
1 1-inch piece fresh ginger, peeled and chopped
1 package broccoli slaw (about 12 ounces)
1 tablespoon soy sauce
Salt and freshly ground black pepper to taste

Heat the oil in a large skillet over medium-high heat. Add the garlic and ginger and sauté for 1 minute. Add the broccoli slaw and soy sauce. Stir-fry for 3 to 4 minutes. The broccoli will still be slightly crisp. Add salt and pepper to taste.

Barbecue Shrimp Easy-Style

SERVES 4

When the Green Turtle Inn's executive chef, Andy Niedenethal, cooked for President Bush, Sr., the president declared Andy's barbecue "the best in or out of Texas." That's high praise from a Texan. Serve up Chef Andy's barbecued shrimp the next time you have a hankering for barbecue.

He uses fresh Key West pink shrimp. Buy the best-quality shrimp you can find for this recipe.

• •

2 teaspoons canola oil
3 garlic cloves, chopped
1/4 cup blackened seasoning
6 ounces good lager or beer
3 tablespoons Worcestershire sauce
2 to 3 drops hot pepper sauce
1/2 pound butter (2 sticks), cut into 2-tablespoon pieces
Cayenne pepper to taste
32 large Key West pink shrimp, heads and shells on
1 loaf Cuban or sourdough bread

Heat the oil in a saucepan over medium-high heat and add the garlic. Cook for 1 minute or until tender. Add the blackened seasoning and cook for 30 seconds, just enough to toast the seasoning. Deglaze the pan with the beer (add the beer and scrape up the brown bits in the bottom of the pan). Add the Worcestershire and hot pepper sauce. Bring to a boil and cook for 3 to 5 minutes. Whisk the butter into the sauce and let it come back to a boil. Remove from the heat and adjust the seasoning, adding cayenne pepper, if needed. Let the sauce cool to room temperature. Reserve.

Preheat the oven to 450°F. When the sauce has cooled, place the shrimp in a baking dish large enough to hold the shrimp in one layer. Whisk the sauce—it will have separated while cooling—and spoon over the shrimp. Let marinate for 20 to 25 minutes.

Place the baking dish in the oven for 5 to 10 minutes depending on the size of the shrimp. The shrimp are done when firm to the touch, bright pink on the outside, and white, not opaque, all the way through. Remove from the oven and place the whole dish on the table or spoon onto separate dishes. Serve with lots of napkins and bread to soak up the sauce.

Shrimp Mayalina

SERVES 4

Sigmund "Ziggy" Stocki bought a building that was once an outbuilding of a pineapple plantation at MM 83 and turned it into Ziggy's The Conch restaurant. It became known throughout the Keys for its excellent cuisine and the unusual style of the owner. Ziggy insisted on no menus. Each waiter recited the menu and you had to listen to it all. After Ziggy's death, his son and wife ran the restaurant. Today it's owned by former Dolphin football player Jim "Mad Dog" Mandich and Randy Kassewitz, who continue the tradition of great food. Executive Chef Ben Coole gave me this recipe from their menu named for his daughters, Maya and Lina.

Chef Ben suggests you serve the dish over linguine or rice.

• •

1 pound butter, softened
1 teaspoon chopped red onion
1 teaspoon chopped parsley
1 teaspoon chopped scallions
1 teaspoon lemon juice
2 garlic cloves, crushed
24 jumbo shrimp, peeled
1 cup white wine
3 diced pimientos
20 grape tomatoes, cut in half
4 tablespoons crumbled Gorgonzola cheese
4 tablespoons shredded Romano cheese

Mix the butter, onion, parsley, scallions, lemon juice, and garlic together. Heat the garlic butter in a large skillet over medium-high heat. Add the shrimp, wine, pimientos, and tomatoes. Sauté for 5 minutes or until the shrimp just turn pink. Remove from the heat and sprinkle the Gorgonzola and Romano cheeses on top. Let melt in the heat of skillet. Serve over linguine or rice, dividing the shrimp and sauce among 4 plates.

Doc's Shrimp Étouffée

SERVES 4

Optometrist Jim Boilini's first love is food. He has been involved in the Key Largo Cook-off for almost thirty years. When a restaurant became available in the center where his office building is located, he couldn't resist the chance to open his own restaurant. He calls it Doc's Diner, and he actually cooks there himself one or two evenings a week. I found he had added a touch of New Orleans to his diner with this delicious Shrimp Étouffée.

● ●

1 1/4 cups butter, divided use
2/3 cup flour
3/4 cup chopped green bell pepper
1 cup chopped onion
1 cup chopped celery
4 garlic cloves, crushed
3/4 teaspoon freshly ground black pepper
1/4 teaspoon cayenne pepper
1/2 teaspoon Cajun seasoning
1/2 cup chopped parsley
2 dashes hot pepper sauce
4 cups water or clam juice
2 cups canned diced tomatoes with juice
2 pounds peeled shrimp
1/2 cup butter
Salt to taste

Melt 3/4 cup butter in a skillet over low heat. Add the flour. Make a light brown roux by stirring constantly until the color is reached, about 10 minutes. Do not let the flour burn. Place the green bell peppers in a microwave for 30 seconds or place in boiling water and drain immediately. Add the onion, green bell pepper, celery, and garlic to the roux. Cook for 5 to 7 minutes. Add the black pepper, cayenne pepper, Cajun seasoning, parsley, and hot pepper sauce. Mix well. Add the water or clam juice and tomatoes with juice. Stir well. Bring to a boil, lower the heat, and simmer, gently, for 15 minutes. Add the shrimp and cook for 3 to 4 minutes. Add 1/2 cup butter and blend in. Serve over rice.

Shrimp and Grits

SERVES 4

Sitting on the afterdeck at Louie's Backyard just feet away from the emerald green and azure blue ocean with a gentle ocean breeze is a special treat in Key West. This charming restaurant sits practically on the southernmost point of the United States. It was the home of Captain James Randall Adams, who made his fortune salvaging goods from wrecked ships. He boasted that everything in the home was salvaged. It was bought and turned into a restaurant in 1971. Phil and Pat Tenney now own it. Chef Doug Shook has been making kitchen magic there for over twenty years. He uses local ingredients to create bright, fresh dishes that are served in this casual, elegant restaurant.

Using sweet, fresh Key West pink shrimp and slow-cooked grits, this southern dish, Shrimp and Grits, is a delicacy at Louie's Backyard.

• •

2 1/2 cups milk
2 1/2 cups water
Salt and freshly ground black
    pepper to taste
1 cup stone-ground grits
4 tablespoons butter
2 cups grated white cheddar
    cheese
Pinch of cayenne pepper

1 cup diced cooked bacon
6 tablespoons butter, divided use
36 shrimp, peeled and deveined
    (Doug leaves tails on)
3 cups quartered button
    mushrooms
Juice from 2 lemons
    (about 4 tablespoons)
4 tablespoons chopped parsley

Bring the milk and water to a boil in a heavy-bottomed saucepan over high heat. Add a little salt and pepper to taste. Add the grits and cook over a low flame for about 1 hour, stirring often. Add more warm water if the pan becomes too dry. Remove from the heat and stir in the butter, cheese, and cayenne pepper. Taste and add more salt and pepper if needed.

Cook the bacon in a large skillet over medium-high heat until brown. Remove, drain on a paper towel, and dice. Pour the grease out of the skillet and add 2 tablespoons butter over medium-high heat. When the butter sizzles, add the bacon, shrimp, and mushrooms. Cook until the shrimp color, about 2 to 3 minutes. Sprinkle the lemon juice into the skillet and add the remaining 4 tablespoons butter and chopped parsley. Shake the pan until the butter incorporates with the lemon juice.

Spoon the grits onto 4 plates and place the shrimp on top of grits.

Note: you can use mild olive oil and butter instead of all butter. The shrimp takes only minutes to make and should be made last-minute. The grits can be made a few hours ahead and gently heated by adding a little warm water and stirring constantly.

Key Lime Seafood Pasta

SERVES 4

Andre Mueller's Marker 88 at MM 88 is one of the Upper Keys' fixtures. Although he has retired, he keeps a keen eye on the restaurant and stops by often. The Stocky family now own Marker 88 along with several other Upper Keys restaurants. They suggest serving this seafood dish over pasta or rice.

• •

1/4 pound butter (1 stick)
2 tablespoons white wine
2 tablespoons sherry
2 tablespoons lemon juice
Salt and freshly ground black pepper to taste
Pinch dried oregano
Pinch dried thyme
1/2 pound linguine
2 garlic cloves, crushed
2 tablespoons key lime juice
3 tablespoons bottled buffalo wing sauce
1/2 cup diced tomatoes
1 lobster tail, shell removed and cut into 1-inch pieces
12 peeled shrimp
3 ounces jumbo lump crabmeat
1/4 cup sliced scallions

Allow the butter to soften, cut into large pieces, and place in the bowl of an electric mixer or food processor. With the mixer running, slowly add the wine, sherry, and lemon juice. Mix to a thick cream and add the oregano, thyme, and salt and pepper to taste.

Bring a large saucepan filled with water to boil over high heat. When boiling, add the linguine, and cook for 3 minutes if fresh or 8 minutes if dried. Drain.

Mix the garlic, key lime juice, and wing sauce together in a skillet. Add the tomatoes and butter sauce. Place over medium-high heat. Add the lobster tail and shrimp. Sauté for 3 to 4 minutes or until the shrimp are pink and the lobster cooked through. Do not overcook the shellfish. It will become rubbery. Add the crabmeat and cook for 1 minute to warm the crabmeat. Serve over pasta and sprinkle the scallions on top.

Cracked Conch Cake

SERVES 4

Elegant yet casual describes The Fish House Encore Restaurant in Key Largo. Doug Prew and CJ Berwick, partners in The Fish House Restaurant next door, opened Encore in response to requests from their patrons for a white-tablecloth restaurant. Encore has the tablecloths, crystal, and a grand piano, but has also kept the Keys' laid-back tropical ambiance.

"Cracked" means the conch has been tenderized. Ask for it to be tenderized when you buy it or you can easily do this at home. Cut off the orange fin and foot. Slice the conch in half lengthwise to make it thinner. Pound the conch with a meat mallet or the bottom of a bottle. Go diagonally in one direction and then again in the opposite direction.

• •

1 pound conch
1/2 cup flour
2 eggs
1/4 pound unsalted butter (1 stick), divided use
1/2 cup dry white wine
2 tablespoons fresh lime juice
Salt and freshly ground black pepper to taste
2 tablespoons chopped parsley

Tenderize the conch and place it in the bowl of a food processor. Finely chop the conch. Form the conch into 4 flat cakes. Wrap individually and freeze.

Once the conch is frozen, remove from the wrapping. Place the flour on a plate and coat each cake on both sides with flour. Lightly beat the eggs in a bowl and dip the floured conch cakes into the beaten egg. Heat 4 tablespoons butter in a skillet over high heat. Add the conch cakes and brown for 2 minutes. Turn and brown for 2 minutes. Pour off the butter, leaving the conch cakes in the pan. Lower the heat to medium and add the remaining 4 tablespoons butter, white wine, lime juice, and salt and pepper to taste to the skillet. Cover with a lid and cook for 4 minutes. Remove the conch cakes to 4 plates and pour the pan juices over them. Sprinkle parsley on top.

Conch Piccata

SERVES 4

The Key Largo Conch House is a family-run restaurant and gift shop. This recipe, a favorite of the Key Largo locals, was created by Laura Dreaver, owner of this Victorian-style Keys restaurant.

When buying conch, ask for it to be tenderized. Most conch comes to the United States frozen and is either sold that way or defrosted in the seafood case. It needs to be tenderized. Most seafood departments will do this for you. If not, remove the orange foot and fin, cut in half lengthwise and pound the conch with a meat bat diagonally in one direction and then again in the opposite direction. This sauce will also go well with shrimp or lobster.

• •

1 1/2 pounds conch, cut into medium-size pieces
Salt and black pepper to taste
1/4 cup flour
1/4 cup olive oil
2 tablespoons butter
1 garlic clove, minced
1/2 cup dry white wine (Pinot Grigio/Pinot Gris)
2 tablespoons capers
2 tablespoons key lime juice
1/4 teaspoon black pepper
2 teaspoons cornstarch
2 tablespoons water
1/4 cup chopped parsley

Season the conch with salt and pepper to taste. Place the flour on a plate and dip the conch pieces to dust lightly with the flour. Heat the oil in a large skillet over medium-high heat. Add the conch. When the conch pieces are lightly browned on one side, about 2 minutes, turn them over and brown the other side, 2 minutes. Remove the conch to a platter.

Add the butter and garlic to the skillet. Cook until the butter starts to turn golden. Add the wine and scrape up the brown bits in the skillet. Add the capers, key lime juice, and pepper. Reduce slightly. While the sauce reduces, mix the cornstarch and water together. Add to the sauce and bring to a boil to thicken.

Divide the conch among 4 plates and spoon the sauce over the conch. Sprinkle parsley on top.

Herbed Spiny Lobster

SERVES 4

"Spiny lobsters have to be prepared just right or they will be tough," Key West Grand Café chef Paul Menta told me. He has two loves: cooking and kiteboarding. When he's not in the kitchen, he has a kite sailing school and, combining both loves, writes a cooking column for *Kite Magazine*.

Here are his preparation tips:

Lay the lobster tail flat on a table, hard shell side up.

Feel the high point of the shell. Using a sharp chef's knife, place it in the middle of the high point and tap it to break the shell, being careful not to touch the lobster meat. Once the shell is broken, squeeze the sides of the lobster to finish opening the shell. The lobster is ready for the stuffing.

• •

4 spiny lobster tails
2 tablespoons olive oil
1/2 cup coarsely chopped cilantro
1 tablespoon chopped shallot
2 tablespoons key lime juice
2 teaspoons sugar

Preheat the oven to 400°F. Open the lobster tail on the hard shell side. Pull apart. Mix the olive oil and cilantro to make a paste. Add the shallot. Divide the stuffing into 4 portions and fill each lobster tail opening. Close up the shell so you can only see the crack in it. Place the lobsters on a baking tray and bake for about 13 to 15 minutes.

Mix the key lime juice and sugar together. Remove the lobsters from the oven and take the meat out of the shell along with the stuffing. Place on plates and spoon the sugar mixture over them.

Stuffed Lobster Tails

SERVES 4

Florida lobsters are a Keys treasure. The season starts with a two-day sport mini season. It's always the last Wednesday and Thursday of July, and people head out at midnight on the Tuesday before to be the first to catch their lobsters. It's a chance for noncommercial fishermen to bag a few lobsters under strict rules during the two days. The actual season runs from August 6 through March 31. The Key Largo Fisheries sells out daily of every Florida lobster that comes in. Dottie Hill, who started the fisheries with her husband, Jack, gave me her favorite lobster tail recipe.

● ●

1/2 cup herb bread stuffing mix
1/4 cup water
2 teaspoons butter
3/4 cup jumbo lump crabmeat
4 Florida lobster tails
Salt and freshly ground black pepper to taste
Sprinkling of garlic powder
1/4 teaspoon dried thyme
1 teaspoon caraway seeds
2 tablespoons melted butter

Preheat the oven to 425°F. Mix the stuffing mix, water, and butter together in a microwave-safe bowl. Microwave on high for 30 seconds. Stir and add the crab. Mix well. Place the lobster tails, hard shell down in a baking pan. With scissors, remove the thin shell facing you by cutting along each side. Season the meat with salt and pepper to taste and sprinkle with garlic powder. Spoon the stuffing mixture onto the tail, pressing it in place. Sprinkle the thyme and caraway seeds over the stuffing. Pour the melted butter over the stuffing. Bake for 10 minutes. Check to see if the bread crumbs are starting to burn. If so, cover the tails with foil and continue to bake for 10 more minutes. The lobster should be white, not translucent.

Lobster Escargot

SERVES 4

A & B Lobster House has a prime spot with stunning views overlooking the Key West Bight, a part of Key West Harbor. You can reach it by walking along the Harbor Walk. Founded in 1947 by two men whose last names were Alonzo and Berlin, it's still getting accolades today. Chef Phil Heimer won best appetizer at the Master Chef Competition for his lobster escargot. I've adapted his recipe for home cooking.

• •

1 8-ounce sheet frozen puff pastry (about 8 x 9 inches)
2 eggs
1/2 pound butter (two sticks), divided use
4 large garlic cloves, crushed
8 small shallots, chopped
1/4 pound sliced shiitake mushrooms
1/4 cup chopped parsley
1/4 cup sliced cremini mushrooms (or button mushrooms)
4 ounces clam juice
4 ounces lemon juice
4 ounces white wine
12 ounces Maine lobster meat, cut into small pieces
1 pound escargot (snails)
2 cups heavy cream
3 cups diced tomatoes

Defrost the puff pastry until it is pliable. Preheat the oven to 400°F. When the pastry is ready, gently roll out the sheet to measure 10 x 12 inches. Cut 4 circles about 5 inches in diameter. Cut a hole out of the center of each circle about 3 inches in diameter, making a center circle and outside ring. Place the ring and the center circles on an ungreased baking tray. Break up the eggs and brush them over the pastry. Bake for 10 minutes or until the pastry is puffed and golden. Place on 4 plates.

Heat 8 tablespoons butter in a skillet over medium heat. Add the garlic and shallots. Sauté for 2 to 3 minutes. Do not let the garlic burn. Add both kinds of mushrooms and sauté until tender. Add the parsley, clam juice, lemon juice, and white wine. Cook until reduced by half and then add the lobster meat and escargot. Cook for 1 minute, add the cream, and reduce until slightly thick. Add the remaining 8 tablespoons butter and stir to melt into the sauce. Add the diced tomatoes. Spoon the sauce into the center of each of the pastry rings and place the cooked puff pastry circle on the top.

Note: Shrimp works well in this recipe as a substitute for the lobster.

Escargot (snails) can be found precooked in a can.

Salute's Mussels

SERVES 2

S itting on the terrace of Salute Restaurant in Key West, I couldn't help but think this is certainly a special corner of paradise. Richard Hatch, who also owns Blue Heaven, transformed a little-known restaurant into a delightful indoor and open-air treasure. The restaurant sits right on the beach, with views of the beach, the water, and lots of people watching. Richard suggested I try his mussels made with white wine and a touch of garlic.

• •

4 pounds mussels*
2 tablespoons butter, divided use
4 medium garlic cloves, chopped
1/2 cup dry white wine (Chablis)
Freshly ground black pepper to taste
1/4 cup chopped flat-leaf parsley

Rinse the mussels under cold water. Tap any open ones. If they do not close, discard them.

Melt 1 tablespoon butter in a large saucepan over medium-high heat and add the garlic. Sauté the garlic until it just starts to brown. Add the wine and black pepper to taste. Add the mussels and cover the saucepan tightly. Raise the heat to high, bring the liquid to a boil, and let boil for about 3 minutes. The wine will boil up over the mussels and they will open. As soon as they are open, take the pan off the heat. Whisk in the second tablespoon of butter to thicken the sauce. Sprinkle parsley on top. Serve the mussels and broth in large soup bowls. Discard any mussels that do not open when cooked.

Note: Figure about 2 pounds mussels per person. Store the mussels in the refrigerator. The commercially raised mussels available today are cleaner than they used to be. Just wash them in cold water before using. Scrape off the beard or thin hairs along the shell. This is how the mussel attaches itself to rocks.

*Salute uses Rhode Island green mussels. The secret is to use really fresh mussels of the best quality you can find.

Mussels with Chorizo in Garlic Sauce with Potato Sticks

SERVES 4

Sitting on the terrace of the Alma Restaurant at Hawks Cay Resort on Duck Key, I was sipping a cool glass of white wine and looking out at the ocean. It was only natural that I decided to order a bowl of fresh mussels as the perfect accompaniment. I was happily surprised by a mussel dish with new flavors. Chef Tony Glitz served me his Latin-inspired mussels cooked with chorizo and garlic. What a treat!

Chorizo is a pork sausage made with smoked paprika. There are many varieties. Any type of smoked sausage can be used.

• •

4 pounds mussels
1 cup diced chorizo sausage
4 medium garlic cloves, crushed
2 tablespoons butter
2 cups fish broth or bottled
    clam juice

8 red grape tomatoes
8 yellow grape tomatoes
Salt and freshly ground black
    pepper to taste
1 lemon cut into 4 wedges
Potato sticks (optional garnish)

Rinse the mussels under cold water. Tap any open ones. If they do not close, discard them. Heat a large skillet over medium-high heat. Add the mussels, chorizo, garlic, and butter. When the mussels start to open (about 3 minutes), add the fish broth and tomatoes. Sauté for 2 more minutes. Add salt and pepper to taste. Divide the mussels and sauce among 4 large soup bowls. Discard any that do not open. Add a lemon wedge to each plate. Garnish with potato sticks.

Potato Sticks

2 large russet potatoes
Oil for frying
Kosher salt to taste

Peel the potatoes and cut into julienne sticks about 2 inches long and 1/4 inch thick. Place them in a bowl with ice-cold water to cover and refrigerate for 1 hour. Drain well and pat dry with paper towels. Heat the oil in a deep fryer or large saucepan over high heat to 360°F. Fry the potatoes for about 3 minutes or until they are golden. Drain on paper towels and sprinkle with kosher salt. Serve alongside the mussels as a garnish.

Scrumptious Scallops and Mussels

SERVES 4

"When I've had a long day and want something quick and easy for dinner, I make these mussels and scallops," Dottie Hill from the Key Largo Fisheries told me. She's right. This one-pot dish is easy and fast. By the time your rice is cooked, the dish will be ready. Dottie says the recipe is equally good using all scallops, mussels, or shrimp instead of the combination.

Dottie suggests serving this dish over rice.

• •

1 pound mussels
2 lemons
1/2 cup butter
6 tablespoons bottled, chopped garlic
2 cups white wine
1/4 cup drained capers
1 pound scallops
4 scallions, sliced
3 tablespoons cornstarch
1/4 cup water
Salt and freshly ground black pepper to taste

Rinse the mussels under cold water. Tap any open ones. If they do not close, discard them. Slice one lemon and juice the second one. You should have about 1/4 cup of juice. Heat a large skillet over medium-high heat. Add the butter, garlic, and wine. Reduce by half. Add the lemon juice, lemon slices, capers, and mussels. Stir until the mussels open, about 2 to 3 minutes. Lower the heat to medium and add the scallops and scallions. Cook for 2 to 3 minutes. Mix the cornstarch and water together. Add to the sauce and stir until the sauce thickens slightly. Add salt and pepper to taste. Serve over rice, discarding any mussels that don't open.

Bahamian Boiled Fish

SERVES 4

Sheila Sands is a fifth-generation Conch. Her family were sponge fishermen in Key West for generations. She told me they would make a fish boil with the fish her father brought home from a day on the water. "Most islanders have two jobs and no time to cook elaborate dinners," she mentioned, "and this dish is quick and easy." The recipe changed with the ingredients available. Sometimes it was made with rice and other times with potatoes. She mentioned that it was difficult to get and keep potatoes, so her family usually used rice.

Old sour sauce is passed on the side. It's used in Key West as a condiment. It can be found in some specialty stores, or follow the recipe below.

• •

1 1/2 pounds firm white fish fillets (grouper, mahimahi, cod, or other thick white fish)
1/2 lemon
Salt and freshly ground black pepper to taste
1 tablespoon butter
4 cups water
1 cup diced onion
1 cup diced green bell pepper
2 or 3 bird peppers* (the heat is up to you)
1/4 cup long-grain white rice

Wash the fish and squeeze the lemon juice over the fillets. Sprinkle with salt and pepper to taste. Add the butter, water, onion, green bell pepper, bird peppers, and rice to a large saucepan. Bring the water to a boil over high heat and cook for 8 minutes. Add the fish and reduce the heat to a simmer. Cover with a lid and simmer gently for 6 to 7 minutes or until the fish is cooked through. The flesh will flake easily. Do not boil the water or the fish will become tough. Serve old sour sauce at the table to sprinkle over the fish.

Old Sour Sauce

2 cups lime juice
1 tablespoon salt
2 bird peppers* (optional)

Combine the ingredients and let sit in the refrigerator for at least 2 weeks. Use as a condiment on fish or chicken.

*These are small hot peppers, less than 1 inch long and very hot. Any type of hot pepper or hot pepper sauce can be used instead.

Alma's Ocean Bounty

SERVES 4

This seafood stew looks as pretty as it tastes. Chef Wolfgang Birk from Alma Restaurant at Hawks Cay Resort on Duck Key created this dish from the seafood bounty of the waters surrounding them. His creative recipes are as attractive as they are delicious.

Make the sauce and rice first and then complete the recipe. Hot chili paste can be substituted for the red curry paste. Use it sparingly depending on the type of paste. Boniato is a type of white-fleshed sweet potato. Other types of sweet potato can be used. Chayote looks like a green gnarled pear and is a member of the squash family. Squash can be substituted.

• •

Lemongrass Sauce

2 tablespoons olive oil
1 1/2 cups sliced shallots
1 cup sliced lemongrass
9 whole, peeled garlic cloves
3/4 tablespoon red curry paste
3 cups canned coconut milk
Salt

Heat the oil in a large saucepan over medium-high heat. Add the shallots, lemongrass, and garlic. Sauté for 2 minutes. Add the red curry paste and stir into the vegetables. Add the coconut milk. Bring to a simmer, lower the heat to medium, and cover with a lid. Simmer for 15 minutes. Pour into a blender jar and blend to puree the ingredients. Strain and set aside.

Jasmine Rice

2 tablespoons olive oil
1 cup jasmine rice
2 cinnamon sticks
4 cups water

Heat the olive oil in a large skillet over medium-high heat. Add the rice and sauté for 1 minute. Add the cinnamon sticks and water. Bring to a simmer, lower the heat to medium, and cover with a lid. Cook for 15 minutes. Check to see if more water is needed. Cook for another 5 minutes. Remove the cinnamon stick and add salt and pepper to taste.

Vegetables

2 cups boniato cubes, peeled and cut into 1/2-inch cubes
2 cups chayote cubes, peeled and cut into 1/2-inch cubes
1 cup carrot cubes, peeled and cut into 1/2-inch cubes

Bring a large saucepan filled with water to a boil. Add the vegetables and bring the water back to a boil. Boil for 5 minutes. Drain and set aside.

Seafood

2 tablespoons olive oil
1/2 pound swordfish
Salt and freshly ground black pepper
1/2 pound Florida or spiny lobster
1/2 pound peeled shrimp
1 cup dry white wine
1 cup fat-free, low-sodium chicken broth
8 scallions cut into 1/8-inch pieces

Heat the olive oil in a large skillet over medium-high heat. Add the swordfish and sauté for 4 minutes. Turn and sauté for 3 minutes for a 3/4-inch-thick fish. Remove to a plate and sprinkle with salt and pepper to taste. Remove the lobster from the shell and add to the skillet. Sauté for 2 minutes. Add the shrimp and continue to sauté the seafood, turning it over a few times as it cooks. Sauté for 2 minutes or until the shrimp and lobster turn pink. Remove to the plate with the swordfish and sprinkle with salt and pepper to taste. Raise the heat to high and add the wine. Reduce the wine by half. Add the chicken broth and continue to reduce the liquid by half. Add the lemongrass sauce to the skillet and simmer for 2 minutes.

Place the rice in 4 large soup dishes or on a large dinner plate. Add the vegetables and seafood to the dishes, and pour the sauce over them.

Heavenly Hogfish and Tomatoes

SERVES 4

Chef Charlotte Miller from Tom's Harbor House at Hawks Cay Resort on Duck Key loves to go fishing on the boats from the marina behind her restaurant. She also loves to cook the fish she catches. Hogfish is a very delicate fish. The fillets are thin and become rubbery if overcooked . Chef Charlotte cooks her hogfish fillets on one side only. This way they develop a crisp crust and remain creamy inside.

Any type of delicate white fish fillet, such as flounder, can be used. A general rule for cooking fish is about 8 minutes per inch of thickness. This amount of time will prevent overcooking. The fish will continue to cook slightly after it is removed from the heat.

• •

1/4 cup plus 2 tablespoons butter, divided use
1 1/2 pounds hogfish fillets
Juice from 1 lemon
Salt and freshly ground black pepper to taste
2 tablespoons chopped chives
6 garlic cloves, crushed
1/2 cup sliced shallots
2 cups diced tomatoes, about 1/4 inch
1/4 cup white wine
1 tablespoon mango puree* (optional)

Heat 1/4 cup butter in a large skillet over medium-high heat. Add the hogfish and sauté for 4 minutes. Remove to a plate, drizzle the lemon juice over the fillets, and season with salt and pepper to taste. Sprinkle with the chopped chives. Cover with foil to keep warm.

Add the remaining 2 tablespoons butter to the same skillet. Add the garlic and shallots. Sauté for 1 minute. Add the white wine. Cook for 1 minute. Add the tomatoes and cook for 2 minutes or until the liquid is absorbed. Stir in the mango puree. Add salt and pepper to taste. Divide the hogfish among 4 plates and spoon the tomatoes over the top and on the side.

*Mango puree can be found frozen in some markets. Pureed pineapple or ripe peaches can be used instead.

Dottie Hill's Hog Snapper

SERVES 4

I first met Dottie Hill while researching my book, *Keys Cuisine*. Her Baked Hog Snapper (also known as hogfish) was delicious. I recently talked with her at her Key Largo Fisheries. She said, "I've changed the recipe to speed it up by using a microwave oven. I'm too busy to wait for the oven." Here's her new method.

• •

2 pounds hog snapper or any white fish fillets
2 tablespoons canola oil
2 garlic cloves, crushed
1 tablespoon dried thyme
Salt and freshly ground black pepper to taste
1 sliced green bell pepper
2 sliced tomatoes
1 medium onion, sliced
1/2 cup white wine, divided use
4 slices Provolone cheese

Place the fish fillets in one layer in a microwave-safe baking dish. Test to make sure the dish fits into your microwave oven. Mix the oil and garlic together. Drizzle over the fish. Sprinkle with the thyme and salt and pepper to taste. Place the green pepper, tomatoes, and onion over the fish. Pour 1/4 cup white wine into the dish. Microwave on high for 5 minutes. Remove and pour or spoon out the white wine. Add the remaining 1/4 cup white wine and cover the fish with the Provolone slices. Microwave for 2 more minutes or until the cheese melts. Serve immediately.

Macadamia Nut–Crusted Hogfish with Jean's Famous Mango Sauce

SERVES 4

Kaiyo restaurant in Islamorada is a little gem serving what they call Florida-infused Asian cuisine. This light and simple hogfish dish was created by Chef Michael Ledwith. He told me his sous chef, Jean, is the king of savory chutneys and sauces.

Yuzu is an Asian citrus fruit. It's tart and tastes like a mixture of grapefruit and orange flavors. If you can't find yuzu, two tablespoons lime juice mixed with 1/2 tablespoon honey will work well as a substitute.

Any type of delicate white fish fillet, such as flounder, can be used. A general rule for cooking fish is about 8 minutes per inch of thickness. This amount of time will prevent overcooking. The fish will continue to cook slightly after it is removed from the heat.

• •

2 pounds hogfish fillets
Salt and freshly ground black pepper to taste
1 egg
1/4 cup milk
1/2 cup flour
1/2 cup panko (Japanese-style bread crumbs)
1/2 cup macadamia nuts (lightly toasted and chopped)
1 cup canola oil
1/2 cup mango chutney
1/2 cup mayonnaise
2 tablespoons yuzu juice (or lime juice)
1/2 tablespoon honey

Wash and pat the fish dry with a paper towel. Sprinkle with salt and pepper to taste. Mix the egg and milk together in a bowl. Place the flour on a plate and dip the fish in the flour, making sure both sides are covered. Then dip in the egg and milk mixture. Mix the bread crumbs and macadamia nuts together on another plate. Coat the fish with the bread crumbs, pressing the crumbs into the flesh.

Heat the oil in a heavy skillet over high heat or heat in a deep fryer to 350°F. Carefully place the fish in the hot oil and cook for about 3 to 5 minutes or until the fish is golden. Remove and place on paper towels to drain. Mix together the mango chutney, mayonnaise, yuzu, and honey. Divide the fish among 4 dinner plates and serve with the sauce.

Fish Lazy Days with Key Lime Butter Sauce

SERVES 4

Perched overlooking the Atlantic Ocean, Lazy Days Restaurant is the perfect spot for casual dining with great views of the ocean. The owner, Lupe Ledesma, is there making sure each guest has a great meal. He and his family came to the Keys from Mexico and operate several restaurants successfully. Lazy Days draws a large, appreciative crowd from Islamorada and farther afield for a good reason. Lupe will cook your catch any way you like it. His Key Lime Butter Sauce served over fish or chicken had me wanting to lick my plate.

• •

1 cup water
1/4 cup dry white wine (Chablis)
1 tablespoon key lime juice
1/2 teaspoon garlic powder
Freshly ground white pepper
    to taste
1/4 pound butter (1 stick)
3 teaspoons water
3 teaspoons cornstarch
2 eggs
2 tablespoons water

1 cup flour
2 cups panko (Japanese-style
    bread crumbs)
2 pounds white fish fillet
    (hogfish, grouper,
    yellowtail snapper, sole)
1 cup diced tomatoes
1 cup sliced scallions
1/2 cup grated Parmesan cheese
2 tablespoons parsley

Place the water, wine, and key lime juice in a large saucepan over high heat and reduce by half, about 5 minutes. Add the garlic powder. Add pepper to taste. Cut the butter into pats about the size of 1 tablespoon. Reduce the heat to low. Add one pat butter and whisk until the butter is incorporated. Add another pat and continue until all of the butter is used. Mix the water and cornstarch together and add to the sauce. Raise the heat to medium and stir until the sauce thickens and a few bubbles appear. Set aside while the fish cooks.

Mix the eggs and water together in a small bowl. Place the flour on a plate and dip the fish fillets into flour, coating both sides. Dip the fish into the egg wash. Place the bread crumbs on a second plate and coat the fish with bread crumbs, making sure both sides are coated. Heat 4 tablespoons of the Key Lime Butter Sauce over medium-high heat in a skillet large enough to hold the fish in one layer. Add the fish and sauté for 4 minutes. It should be golden. Turn the fish and sauté for 4 minutes for 1-inch-thick fillets. Sauté 2 minutes longer for thicker fish or 2 minutes less for thinner fish. The fish is cooked when the flesh is opaque, not translucent.

Place the fish on 4 dinner plates. Spoon the sauce over the fish. Sprinkle the tomatoes, scallions, Parmesan cheese, and parsley over the fish.

Café Sole Hogfish with Red Pepper Zabaglione

SERVES 4

While riding their bikes in Key West, John Correa and his wife, Judy, saw a FOR RENT sign in the middle of a beautiful bougainvillea bush at the corner of Southard and Francis Streets. He thought it was a perfect spot for a restaurant. The owner, however, only wanted to rent to someone who made great food. John had to cook for his lease. He had been a chef in the South of France near Marseilles and felt that the Keys climate and native fish suited his style of cooking. His Hogfish with Red Pepper Zabaglione has become his signature dish. He obviously passed the test, because Café Sole opened and has been a success ever since.

Any type of delicate white fish fillet, such as flounder, can be used. A general rule for cooking fish is about 8 minutes per inch of thickness. This amount of time will prevent overcooking. The fish will continue to cook slightly after it is removed from the heat.

• •

2 red peppers
4 tablespoons dry white wine
4 egg yolks
3/4 pound melted butter
Splash lime juice
1 cup fresh bread crumbs
2 teaspoons ground cumin
1 teaspoon powdered garlic
1 teaspoon dried onion
1/4 teaspoon sugar
1 teaspoon dried parsley
Salt and freshly ground black pepper to taste
1 tablespoon butter
4 8-ounce hogfish fillets (tilapia, sole, or sea bass can be used)

Preheat the oven to 400°F. Roast the red peppers under a broiler or on a grill and turn to make sure all sides are blackened. Remove and place in a bowl. Cover with foil and let the peppers steam. Remove the seeds and skin and coarsely chop.

Meanwhile, place the bottom of a double boiler or saucepan half filled with water over medium-high heat. Add the wine and egg yolks to the top of a double boiler. Place over the hot water. Whisk the mixture until it starts to thicken. If the sauce starts to break down or curdle, add 1 or 2 tablespoons boiling water to stabilize it. Slowly add the butter, whisking constantly. When all of the butter has been incorporated, add a splash of lime juice and mix in the roasted red pepper.

Reset the oven to 350°F. Mix the bread crumbs, cumin, garlic powder, onion, sugar, and parsley together on a plate. Add salt and pepper to taste. Rinse the fish and press into the bread crumbs, making sure both sides are covered. Heat 1 tablespoon butter in a skillet over medium-high heat and add the fish. Sauté for 1 to 2 minutes and turn. Sauté the second side for about 1 to 2 minutes. Can be made a half hour ahead to this point. If finishing immediately, place the skillet in the oven for 3 to 4 minutes to finish cooking. If made in advance, preheat the oven to 350°F before needed and place the skillet in the oven for 7 to 8 minutes.

Divide the sauce among 4 plates. Place the fish over the sauce.

Linda's Blender Zabaglione

I make a quick sauce in the blender. It takes only seconds and is almost always successful.

Place the wine and egg yolks in a blender. Melt the butter until it is foaming but not burning. With the motor running, very slowly pour the butter into the blender. Watch the mixture to be sure it is thickening. Stop pouring and let the machine run for a few seconds if it looks too thin. Add a splash of lime juice and continue to blend. Remove the sauce to a bowl and fold in the roasted red pepper.

The sauce should be made last minute. If made an hour ahead, gently rewarm it over warm water, whisking constantly. Be careful, or it may break down or curdle.

Fish Hemingway

SERVES 4

❝We only buy fresh, whole fish and cut it ourselves. That way we know we are getting the best fish," Doug Prew, co-owner of The Fish House in Islamorada, told me. He has a fish cutter who does nothing but cut fish all day. They sell out of hundreds of pounds through their restaurants and fish market. Doug's partner, CJ Berwick, gave me the recipe for this best-selling dish.

• •

> 4 6- to 8-ounce fish fillets (hogfish, snapper, sole,
>   or other delicate white fish)
> 2 tablespoons canola oil
> Salt and freshly ground black pepper to taste
> 1/4 cup white wine
> 2 garlic cloves, crushed
> 1 cup heavy cream
> 1/4 cup chopped fresh basil
> 1/2 teaspoon freshly ground black pepper
> 8 tablespoons butter

Preheat the broiler. Place the fish on a baking tray. Spoon the oil over the fish and add salt and pepper to taste. Broil 5 inches from the heat for 5 minutes. Turn the fish over and broil for 3 minutes for a 1-inch-thick fish. Broil 2 minutes longer for thicker fish or 2 minutes less for thinner fish. While the fish broils, heat a skillet over medium heat. Add the wine and reduce by half. Add the garlic and cream and reduce the sauce by half. Add the basil, black pepper, and butter to the skillet. Stir to melt the butter. Remove the fish to 4 dinner plates and spoon the sauce over the fish.

Key West Snapper

SERVES 4

Riding on his bicycle to meet me at his 915 Duvall bistro and wine bar, Stuart Kemp fit right into the easy lifestyle of Key West. He's the chef/owner of this charming restaurant located in a 1906 vintage Victorian house. He says the Keys have some of the best fish he's ever prepared, which is saying a lot for a transplanted Englishman.

In the summer, Kemp serves his Key West Snapper on its own. In the winter he turns it into a heartier dish with his Parsnip Puree (p.203).

• •

2 cups water
1 tablespoon salt
1 cup thinly sliced red onion

For mayonnaise dressing:
1 egg yolk
1 teaspoon Dijon mustard
Salt and freshly ground black
    pepper to taste
1/2 cup olive oil
2 teaspoons lemon juice

2 cups shaved fennel, fennel
    leaves reserved for garnish
1 cup cored and thinly sliced
    Granny Smith apple
1/4 cup flour
4 6-ounce hog snapper (also
    called hogfish) fillets
    (any type of snapper or
    light white fish can be used)
2 tablespoons canola oil
4 tablespoons fennel leaves

Mix the water and salt in a small bowl and add the onion. Marinate for 10 minutes; rinse and drain.

To make the mayonnaise, place the egg yolk in a small bowl and whisk in the Dijon mustard. Add salt and pepper to taste. When the yolk is creamy, slowly add the oil, a little at a time, whisking constantly until the sauce thickens. Whisk in the lemon juice. Place the drained onion, shaved fennel, and apple in a bowl. Spoon half the mayonnaise into the bowl and toss to coat the ingredients. Add more mayonnaise if needed. Store the remaining mayonnaise for another time. Set aside.

Preheat the oven to 450°F. Place the flour on a dish and coat both sides of the fish with flour. Shake off any excess flour. Heat the canola oil in a large skillet over medium-high heat. Add the fish, skin side down. Brown for 1 minute. Turn over and brown for another minute. Place the fish, skin side down, on a baking tray. Place in the oven for 15 minutes to finish cooking. It's done when the fish starts to flake.

Divide the salad among 4 plates. Place a fish fillet over each salad, garnish with fennel leaves, and serve.

Beach Grill Black Grouper

SERVES 4

The Beach Grill at Hawks Cay Resort on Duck Key is a great place to enjoy great food while relaxing with your toes in the sand. Chef Henry Christian serves this dish two ways. Make the sauce and serve with the fish or serve the fish with a tomato-cucumber salsa. Both options are given. Influenced by his Italian background, Chef Henry serves the sauce over pasta.

Black grouper is a large fish native to the Florida Keys. It's a tasty, firm white fish. Any type of firm white fish can be used.

Grouper is so popular that certain types have become a restricted catch and can only be fished at certain times.

Choice One: Parmesan Sauce

1 tablespoon olive oil
1/4 cup chopped shallots
2 cups coarsely chopped yellow tomatoes
1 cup coarsely chopped Parmesan cheese
1 tablespoon fresh oregano leaves or 2 teaspoons
    dried oregano
Salt and freshly ground black pepper to taste

Heat the oil in a medium-size skillet over medium-high heat. Add the shallots and sauté for 2 to 3 minutes. Add the tomatoes and simmer until all of the juice from the tomatoes evaporates, about 3 to 4 minutes, depending on the amount of water in the tomatoes. Add the Parmesan cheese, lower the heat, and gently cook for 25 minutes. The cheese will blend into the sauce. Add the oregano and salt and pepper to taste. Spoon over grilled fish.

Choice Two: Cucumber-Tomato Salsa

1 cucumber, peeled and seeds removed
1 large yellow tomato
1 large red tomato
1/4 cup key lime juice
Salt and freshly ground black pepper to taste

Cut the cucumber and tomatoes into 1/4-inch dice. Place in a bowl and add the key lime juice and salt and pepper to taste. Toss well and serve over the fish.

Beach Grill Black Grouper

1 1/2 pounds black grouper fillets
2 tablespoons olive oil
Salt and freshly ground black pepper to taste

Brush the fish with olive oil and sprinkle with salt and pepper to taste. Place on a hot grill, close the lid, and grill for 10 minutes. If using a grill without a lid, turn the fish over after 5 minutes. The fish should flake easily and will be creamy on the inside. Serve with the sauce or the salsa.

Grouper Dijon with Champagne Kraut

SERVES 4

Martin Busam came to Key West from the Black Forest in Germany and found he wanted to adapt his cooking style to fit with Key West ingredients and the warm sunny climate. He opened Martin's on Duval. He calls his food German Island Cuisine and says, "People are surprised by my Champagne Kraut, but I just say it's fitting for the bubbly, Key West lifestyle."

Grouper is so popular that certain types have become a restricted catch and can only be fished at certain times. Any type of meaty fish can be used for this recipe.

The base of the Dijon topping is a hollandaise sauce. I make a quick sauce in the blender. It takes only seconds and is almost always successful. The recipe is below.

• •

4 tablespoons butter
1 small onion, sliced (about 3/4 cup)
2 tablespoons flour
4 cups canned sauerkraut, rinsed and drained
1 cup champagne or enough to bind kraut
3 tablespoons dry white wine
2 egg yolks
1/2 pound soft butter (2 sticks)
Splash lemon juice
1/2 tablespoon fresh bread crumbs
1/4 cup Dijon mustard
1/4 cup flour
Salt and freshly ground black pepper
2 tablespoons butter
4 6-ounce grouper fillets

Melt 4 tablespoons butter in a skillet over medium-high heat. Add the onion and sauté for 1 to 2 minutes. Add the flour and blend well. Add the sauerkraut and cook to warm through, about 4 to 5 minutes. Add the champagne and mix well to bind the ingredients together.

Meanwhile, place the bottom of a double boiler or saucepan half filled with water over medium-high heat. Add the wine and egg yolks to the top of a double boiler. Place over hot water. Whisk the mixture until it starts to thicken. If the sauce starts to break down or curdle, add 1 or 2 tablespoons boiling water to stabilize it. Slowly add the 1/2 pound soft butter, whisking constantly. When all of the butter has been incorporated, add a splash of lemon juice. Add the bread crumbs and Dijon mustard. Mix well.

Preheat the broiler. Place the flour on a plate and add salt and pepper to taste. Place the fish in the flour and turn to coat both sides. Heat 2 tablespoons butter in a skillet large enough to hold the fish in one layer over medium-high heat. Add the fish and sauté for 5 minutes. Turn and sauté for 4 to 5 minutes. Spoon the Dijon sauce over the fish. Place under the broiler for 1 minute or until the crust begins to brown. Serve with the champagne kraut.

Linda's Blender Hollandaise

Place the wine and egg yolks in a blender. Melt the butter until it is foaming but not burning. With the motor running, very slowly pour the butter into the blender. Watch the mixture to be sure it is thickening. Stop pouring and let the machine run for a few seconds if it looks too thin. Add a splash of lemon juice and continue to blend.

The sauce should be made last minute. If made an hour ahead, gently rewarm it over warm water, whisking constantly. Be careful, or it may break down or curdle.

Horseradish-Encrusted Grouper

SERVES 4

Tom's Harbor House Restaurant at Hawks Cay Resort overlooks one of the Keys' best sportfishing marinas. Chef Charlotte Miller buys her fish for the restaurant right outside her door. She uses wreck grouper for this dish, so named because they are often found in deep water around shipwrecks and reefs. It's a very large fish with a white flesh and sweet flavor. She says any type of grouper, mahimahi, or thick sea bass can be used.

Grouper is so popular that certain types have become a restricted catch and can only be fished at certain times.

* *

1 cup mayonnaise
3 tablespoons prepared horseradish
1/4 cup flour
1 1/2 pounds grouper fillets
1/4 cup panko (Japanese-style bread crumbs)
Oil to reach 1 inch in a skillet
Salt and freshly ground black pepper to taste
1/2 cup mango or pineapple cubes

Mix the mayonnaise and horseradish together in a bowl. Place the flour on a plate and dip the grouper into the flour and then into the mayonnaise mixture, making sure all sides are coated. Place the bread crumbs on a second plate and dip the fish into them, coating all sides. Heat the oil in a large skillet over medium heat. Add the grouper. Cook for 5 minutes, turn, and cook for 5 minutes for 1-inch fillets. The fish should be golden. Remove to 4 dinner plates and sprinkle with salt and pepper to taste. Puree the mango or pineapple in a food processor. Spoon the puree on the side.

Presidential Blackened Grouper

SERVES 4

A back injury kept Captain Bill Whitney on shore for a short stint. It turned into an interesting time for him. He worked as a chef at Cheeca Lodge and while there cooked for the first President Bush, who was a frequent visitor to the Keys and liked to go backcountry fishing. Captain Bill made this grouper recipe and served it to the president. He says President Bush thought it was the best grouper he'd ever had. After making it, I can see why. The grouper is lightly dusted with blackened seasoning, and fresh salmon is sandwiched between two grouper fillets. The result is a creamy salmon center and just a hint of the blackened seasoning with a surprise hint of fennel. Here's the dish he served to President Bush.

Grouper is so popular that certain types have become a restricted catch and can only be fished at certain times. Any type of meaty fish can be used for this recipe.

Captain Bill made the dish by cutting the grouper into round medallions and flattening them. Fresh salmon is sandwiched between two grouper medallions. He then places the stuffed medallion in 5 1/2-inch rings and places them in the refrigerator so the medallions will keep their shape. You can make the recipe without the forms. Simply cut the grouper fillet and salmon the same size. The result is delicious, if not round.

1 3/4 pounds grouper fillets (or meaty fish
    such as mahimahi or cod)
3/4 pound salmon fillets
2 tablespoons fennel seeds
Salt and freshly ground black pepper to taste
2 tablespoons blackened seasoning
2 tablespoons butter

Cut 8 4-inch-round medallions out of the grouper. Cover them with plastic wrap and pound them flat to about 5 1/2-inch circles. Cut 4 5-inch medallions out of the salmon fillet to fit over the grouper. Sprinkle fennel seeds over the salmon and salt and pepper to taste. Sandwich each salmon piece between 2 grouper medallions. You will now have 4 salmon-stuffed medallions. Sprinkle the blackened seasoning over the grouper. Refrigerate for at least 1 hour, covered.

Melt the butter in a large skillet and carefully add the medallions. Sauté for 4 minutes. Turn over and sauté for 4 minutes. Remove from the heat and serve on 4 plates.

Creamy Baked Fish Fillet

SERVES 4

Charter captain Jim Perry fishes out of Hawks Cay Resort and Marina. He loves to fish and cook. When the fish is large and thick, he bakes it in a very hot oven. He says, "The key to moist, baked fish for this recipe is the sour cream."

• •

1 3/4 pounds fish fillets (grouper, mahimahi, cod,
    or other thick white fish)
Salt and freshly ground black pepper to taste
1 cup sour cream
1/2 cup chopped Vidalia or red onion
1 garlic clove, crushed
1 egg
1 cup plain bread crumbs

Preheat the oven to 475°F. Grease a large baking tray. Sprinkle the fish with salt and pepper to taste. Mix the sour cream, onion, garlic, and egg together in a bowl. Place the bread crumbs on a plate. Dip the fish in the sour cream mixture and then in the bread crumbs and back in the sour cream mixture. Place on a baking tray. Bake for 10 to 12 minutes. Divide into 4 portions and serve on 4 plates.

Grilled Teriyaki Fillet

SERVES 4

Charter fishing boats *Tailwalker* and *Tailwalker 2* are located within some of the best Keys fishing grounds at Hawks Cay Resort and Marina. Numerous reefs and wrecks form feeding grounds nearby. Charter captain Scott Walker, owner of the *Tailwalker* boats, has been fishing at Hawks Cay Resort and Marina for more than thirty years. He fishes only for varieties he can eat. "I like to grill large fish like tuna and wahoo," he told me.

● ●

1 3/4 pounds thick white fish fillets (grouper, mahimahi,
      cod, or other thick white fish)
Salt and freshly ground black pepper to taste
1/2 cup bottled Italian dressing
1/4 cup bottled teriyaki sauce

Sprinkle the fish with salt and pepper to taste. Mix the Italian dressing and teriyaki sauce together in a saucepan. Add the fish and marinate for 5 minutes, turning once during that time. Remove the fish from marinade, leaving the sauce in the pan. Preheat the grill. Place the fish over direct heat. Grill for 3 minutes. Turn and grill for 3 minutes. While fish the cooks, heat the sauce in the pan for 3 minutes. Divide the fish into 4 portions and place on 4 plates. Spoon the sauce on top.

Beach Grill's Grilled Fish Three Ways

What could be better than eating fresh grilled fish while sitting by the ocean with palm trees overhead and a light breeze? The Beach Grill at Hawks Cay Resort on Duck Key serves up grilled fish just that way. Here are three different sauces for grilled fish that you can enjoy at home.

(For tips on grilling fish, see p. 103)

EACH RECIPE SERVES 4

Caribbean Cool Grouper

Grilling locally caught fish is a treat. I know it's really fresh when all I can smell is the sea rather than the fish. Grouper is locally caught in the Keys, and the Beach Grill can pick up their grouper right at the Hawks Cay Resort Marina.

Grouper is so popular that certain types have become a restricted catch and can only be fished at certain times. Any type of meaty fish can be used for this recipe.

Grilling pineapple slices caramelizes them. The sweet pineapple, fresh mint, and a touch of coconut rum make this a pineapple salsa that sparkles with flavor.

Flavored rums can be bought in small bottles or splits at many liquor stores. These are great for the small amounts needed in recipes.

> 1 1/2 pounds grouper or other fish fillet
> 2 tablespoons jerk seasoning
> 4 1/2-inch slices fresh pineapple
> 1/2 cup coarsely chopped fresh mint
> 2 tablespoons coconut rum
> Olive oil spray

Sprinkle the fish with jerk seasoning, pressing it into the flesh. Set aside.

Preheat the grill. Place the pineapple slices over direct heat. Grill for 3 minutes or until the slices show grill marks and begin to caramelize. Turn and grill for 3 minutes. Remove to a chopping board and cut into about 1/4-inch dice. Place in a bowl and add the mint and coconut rum. Toss well.

Spray the fish with olive oil spray and place over direct heat. Grill for 3 minutes, turn, and grill for 3 minutes for 3/4-inch-thick fillets. Divide into 4 portions on 4 plates, spoon salsa on top of the fillets, and serve.

Beach Grill's Swordfish Balsamico

Chef Tony Glitz says swordfish grills up just like steak. He prefers it medium-rare. A balsamic glaze finishes the dish.

Balsamic glaze can be found in some supermarkets. Or, use Chef Tony's recipe here to make your own.

2 tablespoons olive oil
2 cups sliced red onion
1/2 cup balsamic vinegar, divided use
1 1/2 pounds swordfish steaks
2 tablespoons golden raisins
1 tablespoon honey
1/4 cup chopped parsley

Mix the olive oil, red onion, and 1/4 cup vinegar together in a bowl or self-seal plastic bag. Add the swordfish and marinate for 15 minutes, turning once during that time. Meanwhile, pour the remaining 1/4 cup vinegar, raisins, and honey in a saucepan. Stir to combine. Bring to a simmer over high heat. Reduce the liquid for 3 to 4 minutes. Strain and set the glaze aside.

Preheat a grill. Remove the swordfish from the marinade and place over direct heat. Grill for 3 minutes, turn, and grill for 2 minutes for 3/4-inch-thick steaks. Divide into 4 portions and place on plates. Drizzle the glaze over the top and sprinkle with parsley.

Beach Grill's Grilled Fish Pomodoro

Cobia is a local fish that Chef Tony enjoys when it occasionally comes in. It's a firm white fish with great flavor. Chef Tony suggests using any firm white fish, such as mahimahi or cod. He also prefers Roma tomatoes for the best flavor.

1 1/2 cups diced Roma tomatoes
1/2 cup coarsely chopped fresh basil
2 garlic cloves, thinly sliced
4 tablespoons olive oil, divided use
Salt and freshly ground black pepper to taste
1 1/2 pounds firm white fish fillets (cobia, mahimahi, cod)

Place the tomatoes, basil, and garlic in a bowl. Add 2 tablespoons olive oil and salt and pepper to taste. Toss to combine. Set aside.

Brush the remaining 2 tablespoons olive oil over the fish. Preheat the grill. Place the fish over direct heat for 3 minutes. Turn and grill for 3 minutes for 3/4-inch-thick fillets. Divide the fish into 4 portions and place on 4 plates. Sprinkle with salt and pepper to taste. Spoon the tomato sauce on top.

Fish Encore

SERVES 4

Doug Prew and CJ Berwick, owners of The Fish House, were surprised to find that many of their guests were looking for a white-tablecloth restaurant. In response, they opened The Fish House Encore Restaurant and Sushi Bar next to their Fish House restaurant. They wanted to make sure that their more upscale venue still had a laid-back Keys atmosphere. It's been a great success. This is one of their popular dishes. Key lime sauce flavors fish that's coated with bread crumbs and topped with tomatoes and Parmesan cheese.

• •

4 tablespoons butter (1/2 stick) at room temperature, divided use
1 tablespoon flour
2 cups chicken broth
1/2 cup key lime juice
1/4 cup white wine
2 pounds mahimahi or yellowtail snapper fillets (any white fish fillets can be used)

Salt and freshly ground black pepper to taste
1/2 cup flour
2 eggs
1 cup panko (Japanese-style bread crumbs)
1/2 cup canola oil
2 cups diced tomatoes
1/2 cup sliced scallions
1/2 cup Parmesan cheese
1/4 cup chopped fresh parsley

Heat 2 tablespoons butter in a saucepan over medium-high heat. When the butter melts, add the flour and stir until the flour is absorbed by the butter without lumps. Add the chicken broth and bring to a boil to thicken. Remove from the heat and add the key lime juice, white wine, and remaining butter. Stir to combine. Add salt and pepper to taste.

Preheat the oven to 350°F. Sprinkle the fish with salt and pepper to taste. Place the flour on a plate and dip the fish in the flour, making sure both sides are coated. Lightly beat the eggs in a bowl and dip the fish in the egg. Place the bread crumbs on a second plate and dip the fish in bread crumbs to cover. Heat the oil in a skillet over medium-high heat. Add the fish and sauté for 2 minutes. Turn and sauté for 2 minutes or until golden. Place the skillet in the oven for 6 minutes for 1-inch-thick fillets. Cook for 8 minutes for thicker fillets. Remove from the oven and divide among 4 plates. Sprinkle each fillet with tomatoes, scallions, and Parmesan cheese. Spoon the key lime sauce over the fish and sprinkle parsley on top.

Broiled Snapper with Pineapple Salsa

SERVES 4

Little Palm Island is a gem off the shore of Torch Key and is accessible only by boat or seaplane. It's at MM 28.5 and is a dreamy hideaway. Chef Luis Pous, executive chef for the restaurant, creates what he calls "modern tropical cuisine" using flavors from South America and the Caribbean, with French influences. Here is a sample that is simple to make and scrumptious to eat.

• •

4 tablespoons olive oil, divided use
2 tablespoons lime juice, divided use
4 fresh pineapple slices, core removed
1/2 cup diced red onion
1/2 jalapeño pepper, seeded, ribs removed, and diced
1/4 cup chopped cilantro
Salt and freshly ground black pepper to taste
2 tablespoons butter
1 1/2 pounds snapper fillets
4 teaspoons fresh tarragon leaves

Mix 2 tablespoons olive oil and 1 tablespoon lime juice together and brush on the pineapple slices. Sauté the pineapple for 2 minutes in a skillet over medium-high heat. Turn and sauté for 2 minutes. They should be golden brown. Dice the pineapple and place in a bowl. Add the onion, jalapeño pepper, cilantro, remaining olive oil, and remaining lime juice. Toss well. Add salt and pepper to taste. Toss again.

Preheat the broiler. Melt the butter in a large skillet over medium-high heat. Add the snapper fillets. Sauté for 2 minutes. Turn and sauté for another minute. Sprinkle with salt and pepper to taste and the tarragon leaves. Place under the broiler for 2 minutes. The fish is cooked when it flakes easily. Place the fillets on 4 plates and spoon the salsa on top.

Sautéed Snapper Meunière

SERVES 4

Captain Bill Whitney met me at the Hawks Cay Resort and Marina with a big smile. He had just come back from a very successful day of fishing. He loves to fish and loves to cook. He's been a charter captain out of Hawks Cay Resort Marina since 1981. He likes this location. He has access to Florida Bay and the Everglades National Park and the crystal-clear oceanside flats. Snapper, Spanish mackerel, pompano, and grouper are some of the popular fish he brings in. Here's his quick snapper recipe.

Salt and freshly ground black pepper, to taste
1 3/4 pounds mangrove or yellowtail snapper (tilapia,
    sole, or other white fish fillets)
1/4 cup flour
2 eggs
1/4 pound butter, divided use
4 tablespoons lemon juice
2 tablespoons chopped parsley

Preheat the oven to 325°F. Sprinkle salt and pepper to taste over the fish. Place the flour on a plate and dip the fish in the flour, making sure both sides are covered. Lightly beat the eggs in a bowl and dip the floured fish in the egg. Heat 4 tablespoons butter in a large skillet over medium-high heat. Add the fish and sauté for 2 minutes. Turn and sauté for 2 minutes. Place on a baking tray in the oven for 2 to 3 minutes. Meanwhile, add the remaining 4 tablespoons butter and lemon juice to the skillet. Cook until the butter foams. Remove from the heat and add the parsley. Remove the fish from the oven and divide among 4 plates. Drizzle the lemon sauce over the top.

Parmesan-Crusted Yellowtail Snapper with Pineapple Relish

SERVES 4

The Lorelei Restaurant and Cabana Bar in Islamorada provides a great spot to celebrate the sunset in true Keys fashion with drinks, a snack, and the nightly music of a local band. There's always a lively party at sunset. The Cabana Bar sits practically in the water facing west. Yellowtail snapper is their specialty. Rick Jamison, general manager, told me this Parmesan-Crusted Yellowtail often sells out.

• •

1 cup chopped fresh pineapple
1/4 cup chopped red bell pepper
1/2 cup chopped red onion
1 tablespoon apple cider
1/2 tablespoon honey
Salt and freshly ground black pepper to taste
1 egg
1/2 cup grated Parmesan cheese
1/4 cup fine cornmeal
1/2 teaspoon bottled minced garlic
1/4 teaspoon cayenne pepper
1 1/2 pounds yellowtail snapper fillets (white fish fillets,
    such as tilapia, can be substituted)
Salt and freshly ground black pepper to taste
4 tablespoons canola oil

Place the pineapple, red bell pepper, and red onion in a bowl. Toss to combine. Add the apple cider, honey, and salt and pepper to taste. Toss well. Set aside.

Lightly beat the egg in a bowl. Mix the Parmesan cheese, cornmeal, garlic, and cayenne pepper together in a second bowl. Dip the yellowtail snapper into the egg and then into the Parmesan mixture, making sure both sides are covered. Heat the oil in a large skillet over medium-high heat. Add the fillets and sauté for 4 minutes per side for 3/4-inch-thick fillets. Divide the fillets among 4 plates and spoon the relish on the side.

Baked Parmesan Fillet

SERVES 4

Tall, lanky, and with a ready smile, Captain Scott Walker is a well-known charter fishing captain. He works out of Hawks Cay Resort and Marina and owns the *Tailwalker* and *Tailwalker 2* charter boats. His fishing show on Versus television is one of the station's most popular shows.

Here's a recipe he gave me while tying up the *Tailwalker* after a successful day of fishing.

• •

1 3/4 pounds fish fillets (mutton snapper, grouper, or
    other thick white fish)
Salt and freshly ground black pepper to taste
2 tablespoons butter
1 Vidalia onion, sliced into rings (red onion can be used)
    (about 3 cups)
1 cup mayonnaise
1/2 cup grated Parmesan cheese
1 teaspoon garlic salt
2 tablespoons Worcestershire sauce

Preheat the oven to 350°F. Sprinkle the fish with salt and pepper to taste. Butter a large baking dish. Add the onion rings in one layer. Place the fish fillet over the rings. Mix the mayonnaise, Parmesan cheese, garlic salt, and Worcestershire sauce together to form a paste. Spoon over the fish to about 1/2 inch thick. Bake for 25 minutes. Turn on the broiler and place the baking dish under the broiler for about 1 to 2 minutes or until a brown crust forms. Divide into 4 portions and serve on 4 plates.

Snapper Rangoon

SERVES 4

Bananas, mangoes, and papayas, are all grown in the Keys area. Andre Mueller created his Snapper Rangoon based on these local ingredients and combines them with any type of white fish — snapper, yellowtail, or mahimahi. It became one of his signature dishes.

Andre Mueller came to the Keys in the 1960s and founded his restaurant, Marker 88, in 1978. It quickly became one of the top restaurants in the Upper Keys. Although he sold the restaurant in 2003, he still comes in often to see how it is doing. Snapper Rangoon remains on the menu.

• •

2 pounds snapper or other white fish fillets
2 tablespoons lime juice
1 tablespoon Worcestershire sauce
1/2 teaspoon salt
1/2 teaspoon white pepper
2 eggs

2 tablespoons milk
2 tablespoons canola oil
1/2 cup flour
1/2 teaspoon cinnamon
2 tablespoons clarified butter (see glossary) or
1 tablespoon butter and 1 tablespoon oil

Preheat the oven to 450°F. Sprinkle the fish with the lime juice, Worcestershire, salt, and pepper. Combine the eggs, milk, and oil in a bowl. In a second bowl combine the flour and cinnamon. Dip the fish in the flour, then in the egg mixture. Heat the clarified butter in a skillet over medium-high heat and sauté the fish on one side only for 2 minutes. Place the fillets on a baking sheet, browned side up, and bake for 8 minutes. While the fish bakes, make the sauce. Remove from oven. Place the fish on a warmed serving platter or individual dishes and spoon the sauce over the top.

Rangoon Sauce

4 tablespoons butter (1/2 stick)
1/2 cup each diced banana, pineapple, papaya, and mango
1/2 tablespoon red currant jelly

Melt the butter in a skillet over medium heat and add the diced fruit. Turn the fruit carefully with a fork to keep it from breaking up. Cream the jelly with a spoon to

Parmesan-Crusted Mutton Snapper

SERVES 4

Charter captain Jim Perry docked at Hawks Cay Resort and Marina with a boatload of fish. One large fish I had never seen before. It was an African pompano. He explained that it was not African but an excellent eating fish high in omega-3 fatty acids.

I watched him skillfully fillet a beautiful mutton snapper. "It's one of the best eating fish that swims," he told me. Here's his recipe.

● ●

1 3/4 pounds mutton snapper fillets (any white fish fillet
    will work)
Salt and freshly ground black pepper to taste
1 egg
1/4 cup milk
1/4 cup flour
1/4 cup plain bread crumbs
6 tablespoons grated Parmesan cheese
1 teaspoon jerk seasoning
Canola oil for frying

Sprinkle the fish with salt and pepper to taste. Mix the egg and milk together in a bowl. Place the flour on a plate. Mix the bread crumbs, Parmesan cheese, and jerk seasoning together on a second plate. Dip the fillets into the flour, making sure both sides are coated. Dip the fillets in the egg wash and then in the bread crumb mixture. Heat the oil in a deep fryer or saucepan to 350°F over high heat. Fry the fish for about 2 minutes or until golden. Divide into 4 portions and place on 4 plates.

Mahimahi Chardonnay

SERVES 4

Dorothy and George Hertel bought the Islamorada Fish Company in 1984. They first opened a fish market selling the wonderful fresh fish abundantly available and then opened a small café/restaurant. At one time you could sit by the water and watch the sponge boats go by. The Hertels have since sold the company and retired. It's now been expanded into a large complex overlooking the bay in Islamorada, with many smaller outlets throughout the United States. The restaurant is a lively, fun place to dine. Here is their Dolphin Chardonnay recipe.

3 tablespoons butter, divided use
1 tablespoon flour
1/2 cup chopped shallots
1/4 cup chardonnay wine
3/4 cup heavy cream
Salt and freshly ground black pepper to taste
1/2 chicken bouillon cube
2 cups sliced button mushrooms
2 cups diced tomatoes
4 8-ounce mahimahi fillets

Melt 2 tablespoons butter in a small saucepan over medium-high heat. Make a roux by adding flour and stirring until smooth without lumps. Set aside.

Melt the remaining 1 tablespoon butter in a second skillet over medium-high heat and add the shallots. Sauté until soft, not brown, about 1 to 2 minutes. Add the wine and bring to a simmer. Add the cream, salt and pepper to taste, and bouillon cube. Add the mushrooms and tomatoes. Bring to a simmer and stir in the roux to thicken the sauce.

Add the fish to the sauce. Sauté 3 minutes per side, stirring the sauce as the fish cooks. Serve the fish on a plate and spoon some sauce over each portion.

Keys Sunshine Salsa and Sautéed Fish

SERVES 4

Fishing captain Matt Bellinger pulled into the dock at the Hawks Cay Resort and Marina after a very successful day of fishing. He's a flats and backcountry fishing expert. This exciting type of fishing requires an experienced guide and a specialized boat designed for shallow waters and to protect the sensitive ecological systems. Captain Matt loves to cook and has friends over often. He makes his Keys Sunshine Salsa for them. They always ask for his recipe. He says, "No one can make it like mine," but he gave me his recipe anyway. I took up the challenge and it tastes great. It's perfect for serving over fish and on its own with chips.

Captain Matt serves his salsa over whatever fish he's caught that day. Snook is one of his favorites. It is a fish protected by the Florida Keys and has a five-month-long season — September 1 – December 1 and March 1 – May 1. He also serves his salsa with grouper and mahimahi.

• •

1 28-ounce can whole tomatoes with juice (about 3 cups)
2 tablespoons key lime juice
1/2 cup chopped cilantro
5 garlic cloves, crushed
Salt and freshly ground black pepper to taste

1 1/2 cups diced sweet onion (Vidalia or red onion)
1 cup sliced scallions
2 tablespoons seeded, chopped jalapeño pepper

Place all the ingredients in a saucepan and bring to a simmer over medium-high heat. Stir to combine the ingredients, breaking the whole tomatoes with the edge of a spoon. Reduce by about 1/3.

Sautéed Fish

1 tablespoon blackened seasoning
1 3/4 pounds fish fillets
1 tablespoon olive oil
1 tablespoon butter

Sprinkle the blackened seasoning over the fillets. Heat the oil and butter in a large skillet over medium-high heat. Add the fish and sauté for 2 minutes and add the salsa. Continue to sauté for 4 to 5 minutes for 3/4-inch-thick fillets. Divide the fish into 4 portions and place on 4 plates. Serve the fish with the sauce spooned on top.

Captain Josh's Grilled Fish Fillet

SERVES 4

Hawks Cay Resort and Marina is home to some of the top fishing guides in the Keys. Fishing captain Josh Ardis likes to grill the fish he catches. He gave me a simple tip for grilling fresh fish. Place the fillets skin side down over medium-low heat for 10 to 15 minutes. He says the lower the heat the better. He uses a grill with a cover.

• •

4 6- to 8-ounce fish fillets with skin on
1 tablespoon key lime juice
1 tablespoon Old Bay seasoning
Salt and freshly ground black pepper to taste

Preheat the grill to medium-low. Rinse the fish and pat dry with paper towel. Sprinkle the meat side with the key lime juice, Old Bay seasoning, and salt and pepper to taste. Place on clean grill grates, skin side down, over medium-low heat. Cover the grill and cook for 10 to 15 minutes depending on the size of the fillet. If there is no grill cover, grill for 7 minutes and turn over for 3 minutes. The fish is done when the flesh flakes easily. Remove from the grill and serve.

Tuna Confit

SERVES 4

"Cook tuna all the way through and use it in many dishes" was the advice given to me by Chef Charlotte Miller from Tom's Harbor House at Hawks Cay Resort on Duck Key. Her tuna is moist and flavorful, and here's how she makes it and her tuna puttanesca.

· ·

1 1/2 pounds fresh tuna steaks (blackfin if possible)
Zest from 4 lemons
4 sprigs fresh thyme
1 1/2 cups canola oil

Add the lemon zest, thyme, and oil to a saucepan and bring to a simmer over medium heat for about 2 minutes. Set aside to cool.

Preheat oven to 300°F. Place the tuna in a small casserole dish and cover with the lemon oil. Bake in the oven for 30 minutes. Remove and let cool in the oil. The tuna may be slightly rose color when sliced. Use here and also for Salade Niçoise (p. 178) and Tuna Tacos (p. 193). The tuna will keep for several days in the refrigerator.

Tuna Puttanesca

1 1/2 pounds Charlotte's cooked tuna
1/2 pound linguine
2 tablespoons olive oil, divided use
Salt and freshly ground black pepper to taste
1/2 cup sliced onion
2 garlic cloves, crushed
2 cups bottled marinara sauce
1/4 cup drained capers
1/2 cup black olives
1/4 cup chopped fresh basil

Flake the tuna with a fork and set aside. Bring a large saucepan filled with water to a boil over high heat. Add the linguine and cook for 8 minutes for dry pasta and 3 minutes for fresh pasta. Drain and toss with 1 tablespoon olive oil and salt and pepper to taste.

Heat the remaining 1 tablespoon oil in a skillet over medium-high heat and add the onion and garlic. Sauté for 1 minute. Add the marinara sauce and heat for 2 minutes. Add the tuna, capers, and olives and toss to warm through, about 2 to 3 minutes. Add the linguine to the skillet and toss with the sauce. Divide among 4 plates and sprinkle the basil on top.

Basque-Style Tuna

SERVES 4

Jose Palomino opened his Spanish Gardens restaurant in Islamorada based on his motto: simplicity, high-quality, and clean food. He uses organic ingredients, fresh fish, grass-fed beef, and the best quality rice and condiments imported from Spain. He's there to greet everyone, and his enthusiasm for his cuisine is contagious.

• •

1 cup extra-virgin olive oil, divided use
2 large sweet onions, thinly sliced (about 6 cups)
1/4 cup lemon juice
Pinch coarse sea salt
2 pounds yellowfin (ahi) tuna
1/2 cup brandy
Salt and freshly ground black pepper to taste
1 1/3 cups bottled roasted red peppers, sliced

Heat 1/2 cup olive oil in a skillet over medium heat. Add the onions and gently sauté for 15 to 20 minutes until golden.

Meanwhile, place the remaining 1/2 cup olive oil, lemon juice, and coarse salt in a self-seal plastic bag. Add the tuna and marinate for 10 minutes, turning once during that time.

When the onions are golden, add the brandy and flambé.* If using a gas stove, tip the skillet to light the brandy and immediately remove the skillet from the heat. If using an electric stove, heat the brandy for a few seconds and remove the skillet from the heat. Add a lighted match to the skillet and flambé. Remove the match.

When ready to serve, remove the tuna from the marinade. Heat a heavy-bottomed (cast-iron, if possible) skillet over high heat. The skillet must be very hot. Add the tuna and sear for 1 minute on each side for rare tuna. Season with salt and pepper to taste. For medium-rare, remove the skillet from the heat and cover with a lid. Let sit for 1 minute or longer if desired.

Place the tuna on 4 plates and spoon the onions on top. Arrange the roasted pepper over onions.

* Always have a lid nearby as a safety precaution.

Swordfish with Mango Barbecue Sauce and Sweet Plantain Mash

SERVES 4

Morada Bay Beach Café sits on the beach in Islamorada on the bay side facing west. You can soak up the sun or watch the sunset while dining outside. Chef David Peck does a lot of grilling on the open grills there. He makes his own barbecue sauce with local tomatoes and mangoes and serves it over fish or chicken.

● ●

4 ripe plantains
1/4 cup brown sugar
2 tablespoons dark rum
4 tablespoons butter
Salt and freshly ground black
    pepper to taste
1 small ripe mango
1 tablespoon butter or canola oil

2 tablespoons sliced
    yellow onion
2 garlic cloves, crushed
1/2 cup light brown sugar
3/4 cup rice vinegar
2 medium tomatoes, diced
    (about 2 cups)
1 3/4 pounds swordfish

Bring a large saucepan filled with water to a boil over high heat. Peel the plantains, cut them in half, and place them in boiling water. Boil until soft, about 30 minutes. Remove from the water and place in a bowl. Add the brown sugar, rum, and butter and mash with a fork. Add salt and pepper to taste.

Remove the flesh from the mango. Stand the mango on the thick end. Cut in half lengthwise, down the side of the pit. Scoop out the flesh with a spoon. Repeat with the second half. Cut the mango into small pieces.

Heat the butter or oil in a skillet over medium-high heat and add the onion and garlic. Sauté for 2 minutes. Add the brown sugar and vinegar. Cook until the sugar dissolves. Add the mango and tomatoes. Simmer for 15 to 20 minutes. The timing will vary depending on the texture of the tomatoes. The sauce should be thick (barbecue sauce consistency). Cool slightly and place in a blender or food processor. Blend until smooth. Set aside. Can be made ahead and stored in the refrigerator.

Heat the grill and place the swordfish over medium heat on clean grates. Grill for 3 minutes and give the fish a quarter turn to create cross marks on the flesh. Grill for 3 minutes. Turn the fish over and baste with the mango barbecue sauce. Cook for 4 minutes for a 1-inch-thick fish; cook for 2 minutes less for a thinner fish.

Spoon the plantain mash onto 4 plates. Divide the swordfish into 4 portions and place on the mash. Spoon some sauce over the fish and serve the remaining sauce on the side for dipping.

Florida Keys Golden Tilefish

SERVES 4

Pierre's Restaurant combines fine dining with an easy, elegant style. Chef Christopher Gerlach spent summers in the Keys. One winter weekend he came for a short visit and decided to stay. Perhaps it was the thirty-degree weather he left behind in Pennsylvania that helped him make the decision.

Golden Tilefish are found in tropical waters and are not a commercially caught fish. Their meat is firm, white, and mild flavored. You can use tilapia, grouper, or snapper for this recipe. Israeli couscous is a small, round pasta about the size of orzo or rice-shaped pasta. It has a nutty flavor and crunchy texture.

• •

1/2 cup Israeli couscous
4 ears corn
6 tablespoons butter, divided use
Salt and freshly ground black pepper to taste
1 1/2 cups chicken broth
4 6-ounce tilefish fillets
1/2 red bell pepper, diced
2 jalapeño peppers, seeded and chopped

Preheat the oven to 350°F. Bring a large saucepan filled with water to boil over high heat. Add the couscous and boil for 8 to 10 minutes until the couscous is cooked al dente. Drain.

Place the corn on a baking tray and brush with 2 tablespoons butter. Sprinkle with salt and pepper to taste. Roast in the oven for 10 to 12 minutes. Remove from the oven and cut the kernels from the cobs. Set aside 1/2 cup corn. Place the remaining corn in a food processor or blender and puree with the chicken broth.

Heat 2 tablespoons butter in a large skillet over medium-high heat. Add the fish and sear until golden, about 1 minute. Turn and sear the second side for about 1 minute. Transfer to a baking tray and place in the oven for 6 to 8 minutes to finish cooking. The fish is cooked when the flesh flakes easily.

While the fish is in the oven, add the sauce to the fish skillet along with the red bell pepper and jalapeño pepper. Add the couscous and salt and pepper to taste. Finish with the remaining 2 tablespoons butter, by adding it to the pan and stirring to incorporate it into the sauce.

Place the fish on 4 plates and spoon the sauce around the fish. Spoon the arugula and spinach salad beside fish.

Arugula and Spinach Salad

4 tablespoons olive oil
2 tablespoons lemon juice
Salt and freshly ground black pepper to taste
2 cups arugula
2 cups washed, ready-to-eat baby spinach

Add the olive oil, lemon juice, and salt and pepper to taste to a bowl. Wash and dry the arugula and add to the bowl with the spinach. Toss well.

Sangria-Braised Pork Three Ways

When I tasted these sliders at Hawks Cay Resort's Tom's Harbor House on Duck Key, I knew I had to have the recipe. Chef Charlotte Miller happily gave it to me and also mentioned two other ways to use the pulled pork. Here's her recipe along with the alternatives.

● ●

3 to 4 pounds pork butt
1 tablespoon canola oil
3 carrots, large dice
2 medium onions, large dice
3 oranges
1 cinnamon stick
2 star anise
1 bottle red wine
1 cup sugar

Preheat the oven to 350°. Cut the pork butt into 6 pieces. Heat the oil in a large oven-proof casserole. Add the pork and brown on all sides, about 5 minutes. Add the carrots and onions. Hold the oranges over the casserole and zest. Remove the orange peel and pith and add the whole oranges to the pot. Add the cinnamon stick and star anise. Add the wine and sugar and stir to mix in the sugar. Bring the wine to a simmer, cover, and place in the oven. Roast, covered, for 2 hours. Remove the pork from the casserole to a cutting board and shred. Discard any visible fat as you shred the pork. Reserve the cooking liquid if you plan to make the terrine or to rewarm the pulled pork.

Pulled Pork Sliders

SERVES 4

1 1/2 cups bottled mojo sauce
2 red onions, sliced (about 2 cups)
1 1/2 pounds pulled pork
12 minislider or burger rolls

Heat the mojo in a large skillet over medium-high heat and add the onion. Sauté for 15 minutes. The sauce will be absorbed by the onion. Divide the pulled pork among the 12 minirolls. Top the pork with the onions. Serve 3 sliders per person.

Pork Terrine

SERVES 6 TO 8 AS AN APPETIZER

3/4 pound pulled pork
1 cup cooking liquid

Place the pulled pork in a 9 x 5-inch loaf pan. Measure 1 cup cooking liquid and skim the fat from the top. Pour over the pork. Place plastic wrap or foil over the pork and press down. Place a heavy can or other weight on top. Refrigerate overnight.

To serve: Remove from the refrigerator, run a knife around the edge of the pan, and turn over onto a plate. Slice the terrine and serve with cornichons (gherkins), crackers, and grainy mustard.

Pulled Pork and Polenta

SERVES 4

2 1/2 cups water
1 cup quick-cooking polenta
Salt and freshly ground black pepper to taste
1 1/2 pounds pulled pork
1/2 cup cooking liquid

Bring the water to a boil in a large saucepan over high heat. Add the polenta, stir, and bring to a boil. Cover with a lid and lower the heat to medium. Boil for 2 to 3 minutes or until the polenta is thick. Add salt and pepper to taste. Spoon onto 4 plates and place the pulled pork on top. Spoon about 2 tablespoons cooking liquid per person over the pork.

Mary Spottswood's Party Ham

SERVES 40

There have been Spottswoods living in Key West for many generations. Mary Spottswood's husband, John, was a fifth-generation Conch. Their children and grandchildren live in Key West and are thriving there. Their line goes back to the Maloney and Barthlum families, involved in sponging, boating, politics, and real estate. Mary loved to cook and her daughter-in-law, Elena Spottswood, told me that Mary often made dinner and brought it to their home. The whole family loved her food.

Mary learned how to bake ham from Manda Johnson, who worked for the Spottswood family. Everyone looked forward to Manda's ham at the Spottwood parties. Manda used to cook the ham in a brown paper bag. For safety's sake, Mary used foil.

• •

1 20-pound smoked ham with bone
1 cup honey
2 teaspoons ground cloves
1 quart apple juice
1 cup brown sugar
1 cup maple syrup
1 cup mustard

Preheat the oven to 225°F. Line a roasting pan with foil and place the ham in it, fat side up. Spoon the honey over the ham, sprinkle with the ground cloves, and pour the apple juice over it. Loosely wrap the foil around the ham, forming a tent. Place the ham in the oven and bake for about 8 hours or overnight. Remove the skin and fat and score the meat in a diamond pattern. Spoon a little more honey over the top of the ham and add some more ground cloves. Let cook uncovered for 1 hour until it turns brown and a meat thermometer registers 160°F.

Combine the brown sugar, maple syrup, and mustard in a heavy-bottomed pan. Heat over medium heat until the sugar dissolves and the sauce is thick.

To serve, remove the ham from the pan and drain off all of the juices. Place on a serving platter and spoon some sauce over the ham. Slice the ham and serve the rest of the sauce on the side for dipping.

Key Lime Pie French Toast with Berry Compote (page 80)

This special French toast is a perfect start to any day. It's the signature dish at Azur Restaurant—a local favorite, tucked into a quiet corner on Grinnell Street in Key West.

Tom's Harbor House Watermelon Salad (page 177)

Enjoy the color and spice of the keys with a light, tropical salad of juicy watermelon, spiced pecans, and a citrus dressing. It's from Tom's Harbor House at Hawks Cay Resort on Duck Key.

Stone Crab and Artichoke Dip (page 27)

Andrea Morgan from the Eaton Street Market in Key West warmed this dip and served it to me. It was an immediate hit. If I don't have stone crabs, I use lump crab and love it.

Keys Restaurants — From Waterfront Beach Shacks
to Resort Dining Rooms

Mrs. Mac's Kitchen

Beach Grill Soft Tacos (page 192)

With my toes in the sand and a slight breeze blowing through the palm trees, I tasted this barbecued beef taco dish. It's from the Beach Grill at Hawks Cay Resort and Marina where you can eat lunch under the palms or dinner under the stars.

Sangria-Braised Pulled Pork Sliders (page 158) and Alma's Rich Sangria (page 50)

Pork braised in Sangria makes an amazing pulled pork sandwich. The perfect drink with it is Alma's Rich Sangria from Hawks Cay's signature Alma Restaurant.

Alma's Ocean Bounty (page 122)

Chef Wolfgang Birk created this dish using the fresh, sweet, seafood bounty from the waters surrounding him at Hawks Cay Resort and Marina.

Buddy Owen, Owner, BO's Fish Wagon

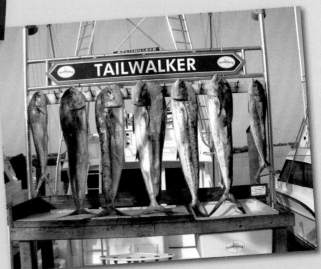

Catch of the day from Hawks Cay Resort and Marina Charter Fishing Boat Tailwalker

Green Curried Keys Shrimp (page 106)

Sweet Keys pink shrimp float on a tangy Thai green curry sauce
to make this delicious Keys fusion dish.

Hogfish Bar and Grill
Killer Hogfish Sandwich (page 190)

Just caught fresh fish, lightly sautéed with a delicate crust, is the basis for this sandwich. No wonder it's an island favorite!

Heavenly Hogfish and Tomatoes (page 124)

Thin fillets, lightly cooked with a crisp crust and creamy inside is a perfect way to enjoy fresh fish from the marina just outside Tom's Harbor House at Hawks Cay Resort and Marina. It's perfect with the tomato, onion, and mango topping.

Presidential Blackened Grouper (page 137)

President Bush, Sr. told captain/chef Bill Whitney that this was the best grouper he had ever eaten. It's no wonder. The salmon creates a creamy center between two fillets dusted with blackened seasoning.

Beach Grill Black Grouper (page 132)

This tasty fish with a cucumber-tomato salsa or a tomato parmesan sauce is a simple way to enjoy fresh fish created at the Beach Grill at Hawks Cay Resort and Marina.

Alma's Key Lime Mango Parfait (page 218)
and Key Lime Cookies (page 212)

Sweet mango sauce contrasted with a tart key lime cream make a light, spectacular end to a meal. It goes perfectly with my Key Lime Cookies. I'm a confessed cookie monster and felt they were a must for the Key Lime chapter.

Dulce de Leche Cheesecake (page 231)

Caramel-flavored dulce de leche sauce is marbled throughout this luxurious cheesecake. It's a perfect party dish from Hawks Cay Resort and Marina.

Hawks Cay Resort and Marina
Charter Captains Matt Bellinger
and Bill Whitney

Sesame Almond Chicken with Mango Banana Chutney

SERVES 4

Jennifer Cornell went to culinary school in Vermont and interned in St. Croix in the United States Virgin Islands, where she learned about native foods and fruits. Using this background, she started her catering company, Small Chef at Large in Key West. It became so popular that she opened The White Street Bistro. I met her in the restaurant kitchen when she was preparing food for a wedding. She told me that this recipe is always a hit at any party. Here it is.

- -

4 8-ounce boneless, skinless chicken breasts
1/2 cup panko (Japanese-style bread crumbs)
1/2 cup crushed almonds (crush slivered almonds in food processor)

3 tablespoons black sesame seeds
3 tablespoons white sesame seeds
Salt and freshly ground black pepper
1 tablespoon canola oil

Rinse the chicken. Combine the bread crumbs, almonds, and sesame seeds in a bowl. Season the chicken with salt and pepper to taste. Place one chicken breast in the bowl and press the mixture hard into the breast on both sides so it is well coated. Repeat with the other three breasts. Refrigerate while making the chutney.

Preheat the oven to 350°F. Heat the oil in an oven-proof skillet over medium heat. Add the chicken and sauté until nicely browned on both sides, about 1 1/2 minutes per side. Place in the oven for 15 minutes. A meat thermometer should read 165°F. Remove from the oven and place on 4 plates. Spoon 2 or 3 tablespoons chutney on top.

Mango Banana Chutney

1/2 small red bell pepper, small dice
1/2 small yellow onion, small dice
1 tablespoon diced jalapeño (seeds and ribs removed)
1 large mango, small dice
1 banana, sliced into 1/4-inch rounds
1/4 cup sugar

1/4 cup cider vinegar
1/2 tablespoon grated fresh ginger
1/2 tablespoon crushed garlic
1/2 cup of mango juice or orange juice
1/2 teaspoon salt
1/4 teaspoon freshly ground black pepper

Combine all the ingredients in a saucepan. Simmer over medium heat until thick, 30–45 minutes.

Caribbean Jerk Key Lime Chicken with Linguine Alfredo

SERVES 4

The Key Largo Conch House is a charming Bahamas Victorian-style restaurant surrounded by a veranda. Walking up the stairs you're greeted by Romeo, their African gray parrot. The Dreaver family own and run the restaurant and make it a very warm and friendly place.

The jerk seasoning for this recipe is very good; however, you can shorten it by using a store-bought jerk seasoning and adding the sugar, olive oil, soy sauce, and vinegar.

• •

1 tablespoon thyme
Cayenne pepper to taste
3/4 teaspoon ground nutmeg
3/4 teaspoon ground cinnamon
1 1/2 teaspoons dried sage
1 tablespoon salt
1 teaspoon freshly ground black pepper
4 garlic cloves, crushed
1 tablespoon sugar
1/4 cup olive oil
1/4 cup soy sauce
3/4 cup white vinegar
2 tablespoons orange juice
2 tablespoons key lime juice
2 tablespoons chopped serrano or jalapeño pepper
1 cup chopped onion
3 scallions, sliced
4 boneless, skinless chicken breasts

Mix the thyme, cayenne pepper, nutmeg, cinnamon, sage, salt, black pepper, garlic, and sugar together in a large bowl. Add the olive oil, soy sauce, vinegar, orange juice, and key lime juice and mix until well blended. Add the serrano or jalapeño pepper and scallions and mix together well. Add the chicken breasts and marinate in the refrigerator for 30 minutes.

Preheat a barbecue or stove-top grill. Remove the chicken from the marinade and grill for 5 minutes. Turn and grill for 5 minutes. A meat thermometer should read 165°F. Divide among 4 plates. Serve with linguine.

Linguine with Alfredo Sauce

3/4 pound linguine
1/4 cup butter
1 cup heavy cream
1 clove garlic, crushed
2 cups freshly grated Parmesan cheese
1/4 cup chopped fresh parsley
Freshly ground black pepper to taste

Bring a large saucepan filled with water to a boil over high heat. Add the linguine and cook for 3 minutes for fresh pasta or 8 minutes for dried pasta.

While the linguine cooks, melt the butter in a medium-size saucepan over medium heat. Add the cream and garlic. Stir in the Parmesan cheese, parsley, and pepper and stir until smooth. Toss with the hot linguine and serve.

Michael's Stuffed Veal Chops

SERVES 4

As corporate chef at Morton's Steakhouse in Chicago, Michael Wilson learned a lot about beef; however, he got tired of the cold weather and fled to Key West. He met Melanie there and made her this stuffed veal chop when they first started dating. She's now his wife and partner in Michael's Key West. I guess his expertise paid off.

• •

1 cup fine bread crumbs
1/2 cup finely grated Parmesan cheese
2 tablespoons garlic powder
4 eggs
4 10-ounce veal chops (center cut)
8 thin slices of prosciutto di Parma
4 large basil leaves
4 ounces fresh mozzarella, sliced or shredded (about 1 cup)
4 tablespoons olive oil
Salt to taste
White pepper to taste
4 tablespoons butter, divided use
12 medium-size button mushrooms, quartered
1 tablespoon flour
1/2 cup sweet marsala wine
1/2 cup beef stock

Mix the bread crumbs, Parmesan cheese, and garlic powder together on a plate. Beat the eggs in a bowl and set aside.

Preheat the oven to 400°F. Make pockets in the veal. Cut slits on the side, entering from the fat side and cutting to the bone. Place 4 slices of prosciutto di Parma on a countertop. Place the remaining 4 slices flat over the first slices. Lay one basil leaf and 1 ounce fresh mozzarella on each pair of prosciutto di Parma slices. Roll up the slices. Stuff 1 prosciutto di Parma roll into the pocket of each veal chop. Dip the chops into the beaten egg and then into the bread crumb mixture, making sure the chops are coated on both sides. Press the mixture into the meat.

Heat the olive oil in a skillet over high heat. Sauté the stuffed veal chops in the oil until golden brown on both sides, about 2 minutes per side. Add salt and white pepper to taste. Place the veal chops on a baking tray and roast in the oven for 12 minutes. A meat thermometer should read 135°F when done.

Meanwhile, heat 2 tablespoons butter over high heat and add the mushrooms. Sauté until they are soft, about 3 minutes. Sprinkle the flour over the mushrooms and stir to combine. Add the sweet marsala wine and reduce by half. Add the beef stock, bring to a simmer, and reduce the mixture by half again. Remove from the heat and add the remaining 2 tablespoons butter to finish the sauce. Place the veal chop on a bed of spinach sautéed with prosciutto di Parma and spoon the sauce over the top.

Sautéed Spinach and Prosciutto di Parma

1 10-ounce bag washed, ready-to-eat spinach
(about 8 cups)
4 slices prosciutto di Parma, cut into small pieces

Heat a large skillet over medium-high heat. Add the spinach and cook until wilted. Drain in a colander. Add the prosciutto to the skillet and sauté for 30 seconds. Return the spinach to skillet and sauté for 2 minutes. Divide the spinach among 4 plates and place the veal chops on top.

Jean Pierre's Grilled Fillet with Shortcut Baked Potato and Zucchini Strips

SERVES 4

Chef Jean Pierre and Diane Lejeune from the celebrated Gourmet Diner in North Miami Beach are retired, but they still cook for family and friends at their Islamorada home, where spectacular views of sunsets over the bay provide a treat for their guests.

Jean Pierre makes his grilled fillet and baked potatoes on the barbecue in his outdoor kitchen. He uses beef loin butt. It's the top of the fillet and very tender. He says any tender beef, such as skirt or flank steak can be used, however. He serves it plain or with bordelaise sauce. His secret to baked potatoes on the grill is to microwave them first and then crisp them up on the grill.

• •

2 tablespoons butter
6 large shallots, finely chopped
1/2 bottle red wine, Bordeaux or California burgundy
1 10 1/4-ounce can beef gravy
2 pounds beef fillet (beef loin butt, tenderloin, skirt, or flank)
1/2 cup olive oil
Salt and freshly ground black pepper

Melt the butter in a skillet over medium-high heat. Add the shallots and sauté until soft, not brown. Raise the heat to high and add the wine. Reduce the wine by half. Add the beef gravy and stir to heat through.

Preheat the barbecue. Brush the beef on all sides with olive oil. Add salt and pepper to taste.

Place the beef over direct heat on the grill and cook for 10 minutes. Turn and cook for 5 minutes for medium-rare. A meat thermometer should read 145°F.

Carve and serve with the sauce spooned on top.

Shortcut Baked Potatoes

4 8-ounce russet potatoes
1/4 cup olive oil
1/4 cup coarse sea salt
1/4 pound butter
1 cup sour cream
1/4 cup chopped chives

Wash the potatoes; do not peel them. Prick a few holes in the potatoes with a fork to let the steam escape. Place on a plate in a microwave oven. Microwave on high for 10 minutes.* Rub the potatoes with olive oil and roll in the sea salt. Wrap each potato in foil and place on the grill for 15 minutes, turning several times. Serve the potatoes and pass the butter, sour cream, and chives.

*Microwave ovens differ and the timing may not be exact. The potato will be mostly cooked and then finished on the grill. Before serving the potatoes, test with a knife. It should slide easily into the potato.

Zucchini Strips

1 pound zucchini
2 tablespoons olive oil
2 garlic cloves, crushed
Salt and freshly ground black pepper
1 teaspoon Hungarian paprika

Cut the zucchini into 1/4-inch strips lengthwise, making sure the strips are all the same thickness. Mix the oil, garlic, and salt and pepper to taste in a bowl. Add the zucchini and toss to coat with the sauce.

Place the strips over direct heat on the grill. As soon as one side has grill marks, turn over and grill the second side just until they are marked. Remove and sprinkle with the paprika.

Grilled Skirt Steak with Candied Plum Tomatoes, Black Beans and Rice, and Chimichurri Sauce

SERVES 4

You can have a delicious tour of the flavors of Latin America when dining at Alma in the Hawks Cay Resort and Marina on Duck Key. The menu offers an array of dishes from across the Caribbean and South America.

Chef Tony Glitz gives a modern touch to many traditional Latin dishes. He turns traditional Moros y Cristianos—black beans and rice—into two dishes: asmine rice topped with candied tomatoes and a black bean salsa.

Chimichurri sauce is another Latin tradition. It usually contains parsley, cilantro, garlic, vinegar, oil, and hot pepper flakes. Chef Tony adds avocado to his.

Chef Tony suggests serving these dishes together or using the side dishes with other meats or fish. The chimichurri sauce will go with any cooked meat, and the black bean salsa can be used as a side dish for chicken, shrimp, or fish.

● ●

1/2 cup plus 1 tablespoon olive oil, divided use
1 tablespoon chopped cilantro
2 garlic cloves, crushed
1 1/2 pounds skirt steak
1 cup sliced onion
Salt and freshly ground black pepper to taste

Place 1/2 cup olive oil, cilantro, and garlic in a self-seal bag or bowl. Add the steak and marinate for 30 minutes. Drain and place on a hot grill or stove-top grill for about 3 minutes; turn and cook for 3 minutes. Add salt and pepper to taste. A meat thermometer should read 145°F for rare. Slice against the grain on the diagonal.

Heat the remaining 1 tablespoon oil in a skillet over medium-low heat. Add the onions and gently sauté for about 15 to 20 minutes. They should be transparent and golden. Lower the heat if they begin to burn.

Candied Plum Tomatoes

8 plum tomatoes
2 tablespoons olive oil
Salt and freshly ground black pepper to taste

Preheat the oven to 225°F. Cut the tomatoes in half lengthwise and place on a baking tray, cut side up. Drizzle with the olive oil and sprinkle with salt and pepper to taste. Bake for 4 hours.

Rice

1 cup jasmine rice
Salt and freshly ground black pepper to taste

Fill a large saucepan with water and bring to a boil over high heat. Add the rice and bring back to a boil. Cook for 10 minutes. Drain and add salt and pepper to taste. Form the rice into 4 balls with an ice-cream scoop and place on 4 dinner plates. Place 4 candied tomato halves on each scoop.

Chimichurri Sauce

1 cup cilantro
1 cup parsley
1 tablespoon fresh oregano
   leaves or 1 teaspoon
   dried oregano
2 medium garlic cloves, crushed
1 cup diced red bell pepper
1/2 cup diced white onion

1 small ripe avocado, diced
   (about 1 1/2 cups)
2 tablespoons rice vinegar
2 tablespoons olive oil
1 teaspoon red pepper flakes
   or several drops hot
   pepper sauce
Salt and freshly ground black
   pepper to taste

Chop the cilantro, parsley, oregano, and garlic in a food processor. Remove to a bowl and add the red bell pepper, onion, and avocado. Toss together. Add the vinegar, olive oil, red pepper flakes, and salt and pepper to taste. Mix well.

Black Bean Salsa

1/2 cup chopped white onion
1/2 cup red bell pepper,
   cut into 1/4-inch dice
1/2 cup green bell pepper,
   cut into 1/4-inch dice
1/2 cup yellow bell pepper,
   cut into 1/4-inch dice
1 garlic clove, crushed

2 tablespoons chopped parsley
3 tablespoons white wine
   vinegar*
1/4 cup olive oil
1 1/2 cups canned black beans,
   rinsed and drained
Salt and freshly ground black
   pepper to taste

Place all of the ingredients in a bowl and toss well.

   To finish: Place the black bean salsa in the middle of the plate. Place the steak on the beans. Spoon the caramelized onions over the steak and spoon the chimichurri sauce over the onions. Place the rice on the plate and top with the tomatoes.

*Any type of vinegar can be used.

Churrasco Steak with Tijuana Sauce and Black Beans and Rice

SERVES 4

Step into Mrs. Mac's Kitchen and enter old Key Largo. Jack MacFarland opened it in 1976 in honor of his mom and her recipes. It hasn't changed much since. That's why the locals call it Keys Classic or Keys Easy. The interior walls are filled with license plates given to them by guests from around the world. This is one of those local treasures — a hometown café serving top-quality food. Angie Wittke started working in the kitchen and now owns the restaurant. She proudly told me that they use only Certified Angus Beef.

Chimichurri sauce is a traditional Latin dish. It usually contains parsley, cilantro, garlic, vinegar, oil, and hot pepper flakes. It can be found ready-made in most markets.

Mojo is a sauce used as a marinade or condiment in many Latin dishes. It usually contains olive oil, a lot of garlic, onion, cumin, vinegar, and sour orange or lime juice. It's sold in many supermarkets in the sauce or ethnic section.

• •

Churrasco Steak

1 cup bottled chimichurri sauce
2 cups mojo
1/2 cup chopped parsley
1/2 cup chopped onion
1/4 cup Cajun seasoning
2 pounds Certified Angus Beef skirt steak

Mix the chimichurri sauce, mojo, onion, and Cajun seasoning together in a self-seal plastic bag or bowl. Add the steak and marinate overnight in the refrigerator.

Tijuana Sauce

1 1/3 cups diced tomatoes
2/3 cup diced tomatillos
2 tablespoons seeded, chopped jalapeño peppers
4 tablespoons chopped onion
4 tablespoons cilantro

Heat a saucepan over low heat and add the tomatoes, tomatillos, and jalapeño peppers. Cook, stirring or shaking the pan until the tomatoes are dry, about 10 to 15 minutes. Remove from the heat and stir in the onion and cilantro.

Black Beans and Rice

3/4 cup long-grain white rice
3 tablespoons olive oil, divided use
2 bacon rashers
3 garlic cloves, crushed
1 cup canned black beans, rinsed and drained
Salt and freshly ground black pepper to taste.

Bring a large saucepan filled with water to a boil over high heat. Add the rice and let roll in the boiling water for 10 minutes. Drain and place in a bowl. Add 2 tablespoons olive oil and salt and pepper to taste.

While the rice cooks, heat a skillet over medium-high heat and add the bacon. Cook the bacon until crisp. Remove the bacon and pour off the fat. Break the bacon into small pieces and return to the skillet with the garlic. Add the black beans, lower the heat to medium, continue to simmer, and toss about for 2 minutes. Add 1 tablespoon olive oil and salt and pepper to taste.

Preheat a grill or stove-top grill. Remove the steak from the marinade and place on clean grill grates over direct heat for 3 minutes. Turn and grill for 3 minutes. Remove to a cutting board and let rest for 5 minutes. Slice against the grain. Divide among 4 plates, spoon some Tijuana sauce on top, and pass the rest around. Spoon the rice onto the 4 plates and top rice with the black beans.

Stuffed Fillet

SERVES 4

Jim "Mad Dog" Mandrich played for the Miami Dolphins in 1972, the year they were undefeated — the only undefeated pro-football team in history. He came to the Keys and bought Ziggy's in Islamorada, one of his favorite restaurants, and changed the name to Ziggy and Mad Dog. It's another winner for him. Executive Chef Ben Coole says this Stuffed Fillet is a popular weekend special in the restaurant.

● ●

1 1/2 pounds beef fillet, center cut
2 ounces cream cheese
2 ounces Stilton cheese*
1/4 cup fresh basil leaves
2 tablespoons canola oil, divided use
Salt and freshly ground black pepper to taste
1 cup diced onion
1 leek, diced, white part only
1 cup diced red bell pepper
1 cup diced yellow bell pepper
1 garlic clove, crushed
1/2 tablespoon brown sugar
2 tablespoons brandy

Preheat the oven to 400°F. Make a pocket in the fillet along the side. The pocket should reach almost to the other side of the fillet. Mix the cream cheese, Stilton cheese, and basil together in a food processor. Stuff the mixture into the pocket and tie a string around in 2 places to secure the filling. Place the fillet on a rack in a roasting pan and brush with 1 tablespoon oil. Sprinkle with salt and pepper to taste. Place in the upper third of the preheated oven. Roast for 30 minutes. A meat thermometer should read 145°F for rare. Remove and let rest for 10 to 15 minutes before carving.

While the fillet roasts, heat the remaining 1 tablespoon oil in a large skillet over medium-high heat. Add the onion, leek, and red and yellow peppers. Sauté for 5 minutes. Add the garlic and brown sugar and continue to sauté for 5 minutes. Add the brandy and flambé. (If using a gas stove, tip the pan to ignite the brandy. If using an electric stove, remove from heat and add a lighted match. Remove the match when the flames stop.) Remove the string, divide the beef into 4 portions, and spoon the vegetables and juices over the meat.

*Roquefort cheese can be used instead.

Salads, Sandwiches, and Side Dishes

The meals I enjoyed as I researched *The Flavors of the Florida Keys* and tested the recipes often included a salad or side dish with local fruits or vegetables or a sauce or dressing with a Keys origin.

Salads in the Keys can be as simple as a green salad with a touch of tropical fruit such as mango and papaya. Marker 88's Tropical Salad with Mango Citrus Dressing turns an ordinary green salad into a Keys treat. The salads can also be more spectacular. Hawks Cay Resort Alma Restaurant's Coconut-Candied Beet Salad captures the pinks, mauves, and greens of the Keys landscape.

More substantial salads can be a light meal or appetizer. Conch salad is a Keys staple. The Green Turtle Inn's traditional Conch Salad gets a kick from hot habanero pepper. Cantaloupe salsa and a sweet and tangy citrus dressing crown Salute's Snapper Salad.

The sandwiches contained in this section make a great lunch or dinner. Choose from Harvey's famous Fish Sandwich, the Original Sloppy Joe, Hawks Cay Beach Grill's Soft Taco, and Hogfish Bar and Grill's Killer Hogfish Sandwich.

The recipes for side dishes are sometimes shown with the main dish they accompany, or they are included in this section. Sweet Plantain Mash, Steamed Coconut Rice, and Sweet Potato Pie are a few of the side dishes in *The Flavors of the Florida Keys*. Pick and choose as you like. I've add Doc's Stuffed Shells to this section. They can be made as a side dish or appetizer or served as a dinner.

Marker 88 Island Tropical Salad with Mango Citrus Dressing

SERVES 4

Marker 88, one of Islamorada's revered restaurants, serves this tropical salad. Most of the fruits are local. Mangoes, papayas, and strawberries are all grown in the area. You can use any type of summer fruit for the salad, substituting peaches and plums for the mangoes and papaya.

• •

Mango Citrus Dressing

1/2 cup mango puree
1 1/2 tablespoons pineapple juice
1/2 tablespoon grapefruit or orange juice
1/2 tablespoon raspberry vinegar
Freshly ground black pepper to taste
1 1/2 tablespoons canola oil

Place the mango puree, pineapple juice, grapefruit or orange juice, raspberry vinegar, and pepper to taste in a food processor. Process well. With the processor running, slowly pour in the oil. The dressing should thicken.

Salad

1/4 pound diced mango
1/4 pound diced papaya
1/4 pound sliced strawberries
4 cups mixed salad greens
1 cup mango citrus dressing
1/2 cup shredded coconut

Place the mango, papaya, and strawberries in a bowl. Toss with the dressing. Divide the salad greens among 4 plates. Spoon the fruit on top of the greens. Sprinkle the coconut over the salads.

Alma's Coconut-Candied Beet Salad

SERVES 4

Alma Restaurant at the Hawks Cay Resort on Duck Key accents this colorful salad with Asian flavors. Chef Tony Glitz cooks beets in canned coconut milk, creating an intriguing combination.

A six-month work study placement in Japan when he was a hospitality student made a lasting impression on Chef Tony. He adds an Asian flair to his current cuisine.

• •

4 medium beets
12 ounces canned coconut milk
4 ounces goat cheese
1/4 cup pine nuts
4 cups fresh arugula

Peel the beets and cut into 1/4-inch-thick slices. Place in a saucepan and add the coconut milk. Bring to a simmer and cook for about 20 minutes or until the beets are tender. They are ready when a fork easily pierces through the slice. Remove from the heat and let cool for 2 hours.

Shape the goat cheese into 4 disks about the same diameter as the beet slices. Place the pine nuts in a skillet over medium heat and toast until golden. Remove the beets from the coconut milk and wipe dry. Reserve the milk. Stack 4 beet slices on each of 4 salad plates. Place a goat cheese disk on each beet stack. Place the arugula on the plate and sprinkle with the pine nuts. Drizzle the pink coconut milk over the cheese and arugula.

Tom's Harbor House Watermelon Salad

SERVES 4

Chef Charlotte Miller from Tom's Harbor House at Hawks Cay Resort on Duck Key was looking for a light, tropical feel to her salad. She saw some pink watermelon and it reminded her of the Keys. She combined it with crunchy, spiced pecans and a tart citrus dressing.

. . . .

Spiced Pecans

2 tablespoons butter
1/4 cup brown sugar
Pinch cayenne pepper
Pinch salt
1 sprig fresh rosemary (or 1 teaspoon dried rosemary)
2 cups pecans

Melt the butter and sugar in a skillet over medium-high heat. When the sugar has mostly dissolved, add the cayenne pepper, salt, and rosemary. Add the pecans and stir constantly for 2 minutes. Do not let the pecans burn.

Citrus Dressing

2 tablespoons lime juice
1 tablespoon lemon juice
1 teaspoon rice vinegar
2 teaspoons Dijon mustard
1/4 cup canola oil
Salt and freshly ground black pepper to taste

Place the lime juice, lemon juice, rice vinegar, and mustard in a food processor and blend together. With the processor running, add the canola oil in a stream. Add salt and pepper to taste.

Watermelon Salad

2 cups seedless watermelon cubes
1/2 cup shaved Manchego cheese (any type of hard
    cheese can be used)
8 cups Romaine lettuce, washed and torn into bite-size pieces

Arrange the lettuce on 4 plates. Sprinkle the watermelon cubes and spiced pecans over the lettuce. Drizzle the citrus dressing over the salad. Sprinkle the shaved cheese on top.

Tom's Harbor House Salade Niçoise

SERVES 4

Chef Charlotte Miller from Tom's Harbor House at Hawks Cay Resort has a special way to cook fresh tuna. She cooks it in oil infused with lemon and thyme. The result is moist, tasty tuna that can be used in several ways. Use her method for this recipe (see p. 153).

Salade Niçoise is a favorite on the French Riviera. Typical ingredients are tuna, green beans, olives, and tomatoes. You can add any other greens or leftover vegetables.

• •

3 tablespoons red wine vinegar or balsamic vinegar
4 teaspoons Dijon mustard
9 tablespoons canola oil
1 pound red potatoes, washed, not peeled, and cut into
    1-inch pieces
1 pound fresh green beans, trimmed and cut into
    2-inch pieces (about 4 cups)
Salt and freshly ground black pepper to taste
4 cups field greens or French-style washed,
    ready-to-eat salad
4 medium tomatoes, cut into wedges
2 cups pitted black olives, cut in half
1 1/2 pounds Charlotte's tuna, cut into 1-inch pieces
1 large whole-wheat baguette

Whisk the vinegar and mustard together in a small bowl until completely blended. Add the oil while continuing to whisk. Mix well to a smooth consistency. Add salt and pepper to taste. Set aside.

Place the potatoes in a saucepan and cover with water and a lid. Boil for 10 minutes or until the potatoes are soft. Drain.

Blanch the green beans: Bring a medium-size saucepan of water to a boil over high heat. Add the beans. As soon as the water comes back to a boil, drain and refresh in cold water. Or, place in a microwave-safe bowl and microwave on high for 2 minutes.

Add the potatoes and green beans to the vinaigrette dressing. Toss well. Add salt and pepper to taste. Place the salad greens on a serving platter. Spoon the potatoes and beans onto the greens, reserving the dressing. Arrange the tomato wedges and olives on the platter. Spoon the tuna over the lettuce and pour the remaining dressing over the top of the tuna and tomatoes. Serve with the baguette.

Green Turtle Conch Salad

SERVES 4

Roxie and Sid Siderius opened the Green Turtle Inn in 1947 and it quickly became a favorite spot for Keys locals. Henry Rosenthal took over the inn in the mid-seventies. The inn has expanded, but the laid-back tradition continues. Several renovations later, the walls are still filled with pictures depicting the Keys of the 1940s and 1950s.

Executive Chef Andy Niedenthal gave me his recipe for a traditional Keys conch salad.

Habanero peppers are one of the hottest peppers available. Any type of hot pepper or hot pepper sauce can be used.

• •

1/2 pound well-chilled conch fillet, orange fin and
    foot removed
1/2 cup key lime juice
1/2 cup orange juice
1/4 cup green bell pepper, cut into julienne strips
    (2 inches long, 1/4 inch wide)
1/4 cup red bell pepper, cut into julienne strips
    (2 inches long, 1/4 inch wide)
1/4 cup yellow bell pepper, cut into julienne strips
    (2 inches long, 1/4 inch wide)
1/4 cup thinly sliced red onion
1/4 cup sliced scallions
1/2 teaspoon seeded and chopped habanero pepper
1 tablespoon chopped cilantro
3 tablespoons olive oil
Salt and freshly ground black pepper to taste

Cut the conch into 1/2-inch pieces. Place in a bowl and add the key lime juice and orange juice. Marinate for 20 minutes. Add the bell peppers, onion, scallion, habanero pepper, and cilantro to the bowl. Add the oil and salt and pepper to taste. Toss well. Marinate for 30 minutes before serving.

Salute's Snapper Salad

SERVES 2

This funky little Key West restaurant with indoor and outdoor seating sits right on the sand. Richard Hatch from Blue Heaven took over an old restaurant and turned it into a place both the locals and tourists love. As we sat on the terrace watching the volleyball game on the beach and beach-goers walking by, we enjoyed his snapper salad with citrus dressing and cantaloupe salsa. It hit just the right spot for a light lunch.

• •

Citrus Dressing

1 cup orange juice
1 tablespoon lemon juice
1 tablespoon lime juice
Core of a pineapple
1/2 tablespoon honey (optional)
1/2 cup olive oil
2 tablespoons cider vinegar

Add the orange juice, lemon juice, lime juice, and pineapple core to a saucepan. Bring to a simmer and reduce to a syrup, about 5 minutes. Place the pan over a bowl of ice to cool. Taste and add honey if a sweeter dressing is desired. Remove the pineapple core. Whisk in the olive oil. The dressing will thicken. Whisk in the cider vinegar. Set aside.

Cantaloupe Salsa

1 cup cantaloupe cubes (pineapple, mango, peaches,
    or other soft fruit can be substituted)
1 tablespoon lime juice
1/4 cup diced red onion
1/2 cup diced red bell pepper
1/2 jalapeño pepper, seeded and chopped
1 teaspoon ground cumin
Salt and freshly ground black pepper to taste

Place all of the ingredients in a bowl and toss well. Taste and adjust salt and pepper as needed.

Snapper Salad

2 yellowtail snapper fillets, about 8 ounces each
Salt and freshly ground black pepper to taste
1/4 cup fresh bread crumbs
1 tablespoon butter
4 cups field greens or mesclun salad
1/2 cucumber, peeled and sliced
1 ripe avocado
1 ripe tomato

Rinse the snapper and pat dry with a paper towel. Sprinkle the fish with salt and pepper to taste. Place the bread crumbs on a plate and dip the fish in the bread crumbs, making sure both sides are covered. Melt the butter in a skillet over medium-high heat. Add the fish. Sauté for 3 minutes; turn and sauté for 2 minutes. The fish should be a golden brown. Divide the salad greens between 2 plates. Add the cucumber to the greens. Slice the avocado and place the slices over the salad. Cut the tomato into wedges and place on the side of the plates. Add a sautéed snapper fillet to each plate on the side of the salad. Drizzle the dressing over the greens, tomato, and avocado. Spoon the salsa over the fish.

Curried Chicken Salad

SERVES 4

T he Zane Grey Long Key Lounge is a beautiful wood-paneled room. It's filled with Zane Grey memorabilia.

They serve their curried chicken salad in a pineapple shell on a bed of lettuce. It's an attractive presentation for a lunch or light supper. The salad is delicious on its own. Add a little pineapple and serve it in sandwiches or on a salad plate.

• •

1 1/2 pounds boneless, skinless chicken breast
1 bay leaf
1/3 cup sliced onion
1/3 cup sliced carrots
1/3 cup yellow bell pepper, diced
2/3 cup red bell pepper, diced
1/2 cup celery, diced
2 teaspoons curry powder
2/3 cup mayonnaise
Salt and freshly ground black pepper to taste
1 whole pineapple
4 cups mixed greens

Place the chicken in a saucepan. Add water to cover the chicken. Add the bay leaf, onion, and carrots. Bring to a simmer and cook gently, 5 minutes. Do not boil. Remove from the heat and let the chicken cool in the liquid while preparing the remaining ingredients.

Remove the chicken and shred or cut into small pieces. Place in a bowl and add the yellow and red bell peppers, celery, curry powder, and mayonnaise. Add salt and pepper to taste. Toss well.

Cut the pineapple into quarters lengthwise, leaving the leaves attached. Remove the flesh from the pineapple and cut into small wedges. Fill each quarter with the chicken salad. Divide the greens among 4 plates. Place a pineapple shell filled with chicken salad on the greens. Arrange the pineapple wedges around the edge of the greens.

Debbiy's Famous Chicken Salad

SERVES 4

Debbiy Doo's Deli and Market in Islamorada is known for its baked goods and great sandwiches and salads. She told me her Famous Chicken Salad is one of her most popular items. She poaches the chicken until it falls apart.

● ●

3/4 pound boneless, skinless chicken breasts
1 cup fresh basil, divided use
5 large garlic cloves, unpeeled
2 cups diced celery
2 cups mayonnaise
1 tablespoon lime juice
Salt and freshly ground black pepper to taste

Preheat the oven to 350°F. Place the chicken in an oven-proof casserole dish and cover with water. Add 1/2 cup basil and the garlic. Cover with foil or a lid and place in the oven for 3 hours. Strain the chicken and shred. Place in a bowl and add the celery and mayonnaise. Mix well. Chop the remaining 1/2 cup basil and add to the salad with the lime juice and salt and pepper to taste. Serve as a salad or on rolls as a sandwich.

"Ancient Secret" Quinoa Salad

SERVES 4

Charlie Wilson opened her organic restaurant bar, Help Yourself, in a small space bringing fresh, healthful foods to Key West. People there are becoming more aware of this style of food and she has had to expand her space.

Quinoa is a tiny South American grain used by the warriors in ancient times to increase energy and endurance. When cooked, it has a fluffy yet slightly crunchy texture and a nutty flavor. It has the highest protein of any grain and contains all nine of the essential amino acids, making it the only grain that is a complete protein.

Charlie suggests serving this salad as a side dish or over simple mixed greens for lunch.

- -

1 cup quinoa to make 2 1/2 cups cooked quinoa
2 cups water
1 cup cooked chickpeas or canned organic chickpeas,
    rinsed and drained
1/4 cup dried goji berries*
1 apple, cored and diced
1/2 cup whole almonds, roughly chopped
1/2 tablespoon ground cumin
1/2 cup orange juice
1/2 teaspoon salt
2 tablespoons olive oil
Orange segments for garnish

Place the quinoa in a saucepan and add the water. Bring the water to a boil over high heat, lower the heat, and simmer for 15 minutes. The liquid should be absorbed and the quinoa fluffy. Place in a bowl and add the chickpeas, goji berries, apple, almonds, ground cumin, orange juice, salt, and olive oil. Toss well. Taste and add more seasoning if needed. Garnish with the orange segments.

*Goji berries are bright red berries about the size of raisins, and they're considered to be "super food" due to their high nutritional value. They have more beta-carotene than carrots, more iron than spinach, and twenty-one trace minerals. Plus goji berries contain 13 percent protein and extremely high levels of antioxidants! They can be found in most health food stores and in some supermarkets.

Black Bean and Rice Salad

SERVES 6

What do you do with leftover black beans and rice? Sally Thomas of Key West gave me this recipe. It's so good that I don't wait for leftovers to make it. The salad makes a great party dish and can easily be doubled or tripled.

• •

2 cups cooked from dried or rinsed and drained
    canned black beans
2 cups cooked rice
1 1/2 cups cilantro
1/4 cup lime juice
3/4 cup canola oil
1/2 cup chopped onion
2 medium garlic cloves, crushed
Salt and freshly ground black pepper to taste

Mix the beans, rice, and cilantro together in a bowl. Place the lime juice in a small bowl and whisk in the oil. Add the onion and garlic and pour over the rice and beans. Toss well. Add salt and pepper to taste.

Harvey's Fish Sandwich

SERVES 1

D riving through the Keys on Overseas Highway you can see many signs that read: "Harvey's Fish Sandwich sold here." It has become one of the most famous sandwiches in the Keys.

Many people love the sandwich but don't know Harvey's story. As a retired, disabled fireman, Harvey went to the Keys and worked as a fish cutter at the Key Largo Pilot House Restaurant in the 1970s. Everyone knew Harvey with his khaki pants and shirt, no shoes, and his ever-present bicycle. In those days, he cut fish fillets for twenty cents a pound and fish cheeks and throats for two cents a pound. Any leftover fish was his. With his fish, some onions, and bread, he would fry up a sandwich for himself. He lived at a nearby boatyard and started frying these sandwiches in large pans for any of the stray fishermen who happened to be around. Soon, people were coming into the Pilot House asking for Harvey's sandwich. Craig Belcher, one of the chefs at the time, developed the sandwich so that it could be sold on a large scale. Within six months, it accounted for 30 percent of the Pilot House's business. It has continued its popularity throughout the Upper Keys. Here's Craig's original version.

• •

2 tablespoons bread crumbs
3 ounces grouper or mahimahi fillets
Oil for frying
1 tablespoon butter
1/2 cup diced onion
1 slice yellow cheese (any type)
2 slices whole-wheat toast
1 tablespoon tartar sauce
2 slices tomatoes

Place the bread crumbs on a plate and roll the fish in them. Heat the oil to 350°F in a deep fryer or saucepan over high heat. Fry the fish for 3 to 4 minutes or until golden. Remove to a plate lined with paper towels to drain. Melt the butter in a small skillet over medium-high heat. Add the onion and sauté until golden, about 2 to 3 minutes. Meanwhile, place the cheese on the whole-wheat toast and melt in a toaster oven or under a broiler. To serve, place the fish on top of the melted cheese on one toast slice, cover with the onions, tartar sauce, and tomato slices. Cover with the second toast slice. Cut in half and serve immediately.

Use this tartar sauce or a bottled one from the market.

Tartar Sauce

1/2 cup mayonnaise
1 1/2 tablespoons Dijon mustard
1 tablespoon chopped onion
1 tablespoon sweet relish
1 tablespoon lime juice
1 teaspoon Worcestershire sauce
Salt and freshly ground black pepper to taste

Combine the ingredients in a small bowl and add salt and pepper to taste. Makes about 3/4 cup sauce.

BO's Grilled Fish Sandwich

SERVES 4

Some of the best fish sandwiches in Key West can be found in a rambling shack known as BO's Fish Wagon. It looks like a hurricane blew it to pieces. And that's happened more than once, but Buddy Owen (hence BO) always nails it back together.

Buddy Owen used to live on his boat and cook the fresh fish he caught for friends. He wouldn't open a restaurant because "it was too much work." So a friend made him an enclosed cooking cart, and he pulled it to a parking lot with his old truck. The parking lot owners weren't too happy, but the office staff in the nearby building loved his food, and he stayed there for fifteen years. The land was going to be developed, so he hitched up his wagon again and landed at the corner of Caroline and William Streets. He shot out the tires on the wagon and truck, and they have been there ever since.

I've adapted Buddy's recipe for home cooking.

• •

1 cup Key Lime Mayonnaise (see recipe below)
2 loaves Cuban bread cut into 4 6-inch portions
3 eggs
2 pounds fresh fish (mahimahi, grouper, snapper, or other white fish)
1 cup cracker meal
Peanut oil for frying
Salt and freshly ground black pepper to taste
Squirt of bottled key lime juice
Several lettuce leaves
1 medium tomato, sliced

Break the eggs into a bowl. Place the cracker meal on a plate. Dip the fish into the eggs and then into the cracker meal to lightly coat the fish. Press the meal into the fish on both sides. Heat the oil in a deep saucepan to 375°F. Add the fish and remove it as soon as it turns golden, about 3 to 4 minutes. Drain on a paper towel. Cut the bread in half lengthwise. Spread the bottom halves with half the Key Lime Mayonnaise. Place the fish on the bottom half of each bread. Add salt and pepper to taste to the fish. Sprinkle each piece with a squirt of key lime juice. Place the lettuce and sliced tomato over the fish. Spread the remaining Key Lime Mayonnaise over the top halves of the bread. Close the sandwiches, cut in half crosswise, and serve.

Key Lime Mayonnaise

1 cup good-quality bottled mayonnaise
2 tablespoons bottled key lime juice
4 teaspoons seasoning (Old Bay or mild jerk seasoning)*

Mix the ingredients together.

*Buddy uses a prepared seasoning in his mayonnaise. Holly Owens, Buddy's wife, suggests using Old Bay seasoning or a mild jerk seasoning.

Hogfish Bar and Grill Killer Hogfish Sandwich

SERVES 4

On Stock Island, old Key West is alive and well. According to the locals, it's "the way Key West used to be: fresh seafood, strong drinks, magnificent waterfront views, and plenty of local characters." Stock Island is separated from Key West by Cow Key Channel. At Bobby Mongelli's Hogfish Bar and Grill, you can sit at picnic tables right on the waterfront and enjoy the freshest fish in a relaxing atmosphere. If you hit it lucky, you'll have fresh hogfish just caught and brought to the dock by Bobby. The Hogfish Bar and Grill Killer Hogfish Sandwich is an island favorite. The recipe was given to me by Chef Jason Wooters.

Any type of delicate white fish fillet, such as flounder, can be used. A general rule for cooking fish is about 8 minutes per inch of thickness. This amount of time will prevent overcooking. The fish will continue to cook slightly after it is removed from the heat.

• •

1/3 cups cracker meal
1/2 cup plus 1/3 cup self-rising flour, divided use
16 ounces buttermilk
4 8-ounce fresh hogfish fillets (tilapia, snapper, sole, or
    other white fish can be used)
2 tablespoons olive oil, plus more for frying
1 cup chopped button mushrooms
1 large yellow onion, chopped (about 2 cups)
8 slices Swiss cheese
3/4 cup bottled tartar sauce
2 fresh loaves Cuban bread, cut into 4 6-inch portions
4 lettuce leaves
1 medium tomato, sliced
Lemon wedges for garnish

Mix the cracker meal with 1/3 cup self-rising flour on a plate. Place the remaining 1/2 cup flour on a separate plate. Place the buttermilk in a bowl. Dip the hogfish fillet into the 1/2 cup self-rising flour to coat, then dip it into the buttermilk. Dip the fish into the cracker meal and flour mixture, making sure to press firmly and evenly to ensure equal breading on both sides. Repeat until all the hogfish fillets have been breaded. Set aside.

Heat the olive oil in a large skillet over medium-high heat. Add the mushrooms and onions and sauté until lightly browned and softened, about 3 minutes. Divide the mixture in the skillet into 4 portions. Remove from the heat. Place 2 cheese slices over each section of the mushroom and onion mixture. The slices will melt over the mixture. Leave in the skillet while the fish is fried.

Add 1/2 inch olive oil to a large skillet for shallow frying. Heat the oil to 325°F. Fry the hogfish for approximately 3 minutes per side and set aside on a paper towel to absorb the excess oil.

Spread the tartar sauce over the bread. Add the fried fish and, using a spatula, place the mushroom mixture over the fish. Add a few lettuce leaves and slices of tomato. Serve with the lemon wedges.

Beach Grill Soft Tacos

SERVES 4

Hawks Cay Resort and Marina is located on sixty acres at MM 61. With 5 top restaurants, you can choose whatever style of cuisine you like. The Beach Grill sits right on the sand next to the ocean. Eat lunch there under the palms or have dinner under the stars.

· ·

Key Lime Vinaigrette

1/4 cup key lime juice
1/2 tablespoon honey
2 teaspoons Dijon mustard
1 teaspoon whole-grain mustard
1/2 cup canola oil
Salt and freshly ground black pepper to taste

Mix the cup key lime juice with the honey, Dijon mustard, and whole-grain mustard until smooth. Slowly whisk in the oil, stirring constantly to thicken the dressing. Add salt and pepper to taste. Set aside.

Coleslaw

4 cups sliced cabbage
2 cups sliced radish
1/4 cup chopped cilantro

Place the cabbage, radish, and cilantro in a bowl. Add the Key Lime Vinaigrette and toss well.

Steak

1 pound skirt steak
1 cup key lime juice
Salt and freshly ground black pepper to taste
4 flour tortillas
1/4 teaspoon cayenne pepper

Place the steak in a self-seal plastic bag. Pour the key lime juice over the steak. Marinate for 10 minutes. Drain the steak and pat dry with a paper towel. Add salt and pepper to taste. Place the steak on a hot grill for 3 minutes. Turn and grill for 3 minutes or until a meat thermometer reaches 145°F for rare. Remove to a cutting board and slice the steak against the grain. Warm the tortillas on the grill for about 1 minute or until they start to bubble. Fill each tortilla with the steak and then the coleslaw. Sprinkle the cayenne pepper on top.

Tuna Tacos

SERVES 4

Chef Charlotte Miller from Tom's Harbor House at Hawks Cay Resort on Duck Key says these tacos make easy snacks or lunches for picnics, boating, or just enjoying at home.

Chef Charlotte has a special way to cook tuna so that it's moist, tasty, and versatile (see p. 153 for the recipe).

• •

8 5- to 6-inch corn tortillas
2 cups Charlotte's cooked tuna, flaked with a fork
8 tablespoons bottled salsa
1 cup shredded lettuce

Folded Tortilla Sandwich

Heat each tortilla in a skillet for about 1 to 2 minutes. Remove and fold in half. Place on a plate. Spoon 1/4 cup tuna into each tortilla, top with 1 tablespoon salsa, and fill with shredded lettuce. Serve 2 tacos per person.

Flat Crisp Tortilla

Heat each tortilla in a skillet for about 3 minutes, turning once during that time. The tortilla should start to turn golden and be crisp. Serve the tortillas flat on a plate and spoon the tuna, salsa, and lettuce on each one as above. Serve 2 per person.

Beach Grill Smoked Wahoo Salad Sandwich

SERVES 4

Wahoo is a prized game fish. It is one of the fastest swimming fish and has a white delicate flesh. A member of the mackerel family, wahoo resembles king mackerel and is considered the gourmet's mackerel. It's leaner than a king mackerel. Wahoo is sometimes sold fresh or smoked commercially. Smoked trout can be used for this recipe.

This is a simple, tasty smoked fish salad from the Beach Grill at Hawks Cay Resort on Duck Key. Serve the sandwich with some chips and tomato and lettuce on the side.

● ●

1 pound smoked wahoo (or smoked trout)
1/2 cup diced red onion
1 cup diced celery
1/4 cup chopped parsley
4 teaspoons lemon juice
2 cups mayonnaise plus 4 tablespoons
Salt and freshly ground black pepper to taste
4 Kaiser rolls or hard rolls, toasted

Chop the wahoo and add the red onion, celery, parsley, lemon juice, and 2 cups mayonnaise. This can be done in a food processor. Add salt and pepper to taste. Spread the remaining 4 tablespoons mayonnaise on the toasted rolls. Divide the wahoo salad into four portions and spread on the rolls.

The Fish House "Konk" Burger

SERVES 4

The Fish House in Key Largo is a happy, packed place. There's usually a line waiting to get in — and for good reason. The fish is fresh and good and the atmosphere fun.

Their "Konk" Burger gets raves from local diners.

Conch, pronounced "konk," has been overfished in U.S. waters. We now get our conch imported and frozen.

• •

1 pound conch
2 tablespoons tomato paste
4 celery stalks, cut into 3-inch pieces
6 tablespoons diced onion
1 tablespoon cracker meal
2 1/2 cups Italian bread crumbs
2 eggs
Several drops hot pepper sauce
4 garlic cloves, crushed
1 tablespoon canola oil
4 hamburger rolls
4 sliced tomatoes
Several lettuce leaves
4 tablespoons cocktail sauce

Remove the foot, cut off the orange fin, and trim off any dark pieces of skin on the conch. Cut the conch into small pieces and place in the bowl of a food processor. Add the tomato paste, celery, onion, cracker meal, Italian bread crumbs, eggs, hot pepper sauce, and garlic. Process until the ingredients start to come together. Form the mixture into 4 burgers about 3 1/2 inches in diameter and 1/2 inch thick. Heat the oil in a skillet over medium-high heat. Add the burgers and sauté for 4 minutes or until they are golden on one side. Lower the heat to medium and turn the burgers. Cover with a lid and cook for 4 minutes. Place each burger on the bottom slice of a hamburger roll. Place a slice of tomato on the burger and lettuce over the tomato. Spoon the cocktail sauce over the lettuce. Close with the top of the hamburger roll.

Mahi Reuben

SERVES 4

Island Grill in the Upper Keys was once a floating restaurant but now has been expanded into a fun, waterside restaurant and bar with live entertainment. Come by boat and taste some great, casual food.

• •

1 cup crushed cornflakes
1 cup pancake mix
Salt and freshly ground black pepper to taste
2 eggs
4 6-ounce mahimahi fillets (any firm white fish
    can be used)
2 tablespoons canola oil
4 large sourdough rolls (about 6 inches long)
4 large slices Swiss cheese
1/4 cup Thousand Island dressing
1/2 cup coleslaw
8 lettuce leaves
4 onion slices
1 dill pickle, quartered

Mix the cornflakes and pancake mix together on a plate or in a bowl. Add salt and pepper to taste. Lightly beat the eggs in a bowl. Place the fish in the egg and then in the pancake mixture, making sure both sides are coated.

Heat the oil in a large skillet and add the fish. Sauté for 4 minutes; turn and sauté for 4 minutes for a 3/4-inch-thick fillet. Cook for 2 minutes longer for a 1-inch-thick fillet or 1 minute less for a 1/2-inch-thick fillet.

Place one fillet on the bottom half of each roll. Add 1 slice cheese on top of each fillet. Spread the cheese with the Thousand Island dressing. Spoon the coleslaw over the dressing and close the sandwich with the top half of the bread. Place the sandwich on a panini press and heat just to melt the cheese. Or, place in a skillet and press down with a lid to melt the cheese. Serve on a plate with the lettuce leaves, onion slices, and dill pickle.

The Original Sloppy Joe's Sandwich

SERVES 4

Sloppy Joe's Bar has been on the same site with many of the same fixtures since 1937. Joe "Josie" Russell opened his speakeasy bar during Prohibition in 1933. As soon as repeal came, he turned it into a legitimate saloon, eventually moving it to the present site in 1937. Josie was Hemingway's boat pilot and fishing companion and Hemingway was a favorite patron of the bar. The story goes that Hemingway said to Josie, "Joe you run a sloppy place. You should call it Sloppy Joe's." Each year Sloppy Joe's holds a Hemingway look-alike contest around July 21, his birthday.

Sloppy Joe's make their own mix for this famous sandwich.

• •

2 tablespoons canola oil
1 cup diced onion
1/2 cup diced green bell pepper
1 cup diced celery
2 garlic cloves, crushed
Salt to taste
1 pound ground Beef
2 cups ketchup
1/4 cup brown sugar
1 tablespoon Worcestershire sauce
1 tablespoon cider vinegar
2 tablespoons tomato paste
1/4 cup barbecue sauce
4 hamburger rolls

Heat the oil over medium-high heat in a large skillet. Add the onion, green bell pepper, celery, and garlic. Sauté until the vegetables are translucent, not brown, about 5 minutes. Add the beef and break up into small pieces. Cook until the meat is no longer red, about 2 minutes. Drain the fat from the skillet and add the ketchup, brown sugar, Worcestershire sauce, cider vinegar, tomato paste, and barbecue sauce. Lower the heat to medium-low and gently cook for 30 minutes, stirring several times. Toast the hamburger rolls and place on 4 plates. Serve the meat sauce over the rolls.

Beach Grill Toasted Roast

SERVES 4

The Beach Grill at Hawks Cay Resort on Duck Key has an outdoor barbecue station and tables sitting right on the sand with palm trees swaying in the breeze above. It's an ideal Keys setting for lunch or dinner. One perfect Keys day, I enjoyed this decadent roast beef and melted cheese sandwich. Chef Tony Glitz shared the recipe with me.

The secret to the sandwich is the marinated tomatoes. They should marinate overnight.

• •

Marinated Tomatoes

2 cups canned whole tomatoes, drained
1/2 teaspoon dried oregano
1/2 teaspoon dried thyme
2 tablespoons olive oil
Salt and freshly ground black pepper to taste

Place the drained tomatoes, oregano, thyme, and olive oil in a bowl. Add salt and pepper to taste. Cover and refrigerate overnight.

Toasted Roast Sandwich

4 tablespoons horseradish
8 slices sourdough bread
24 slices roast beef (about same size as bread)
8 slices provolone cheese
4 slices havarti cheese

Toast the sourdough bread and spread the horseradish over 4 slices. Set aside.

Drain the tomatoes and cut into quarters. Divide the roast beef slices into 4 portions (6 slices each). Divide the provolone slices into 4 portions (2 slices each). Divide the havarti cheese into 4 portions (1 slice each).

Heat a skillet over medium-high heat. Place 6 slices roast beef in the skillet. Cover with one quarter of the tomatoes. Place 1 slice havarti cheese over the tomatoes and 2 slices provolone on top. Cover with a lid and cook a few minutes until the cheese melts. Remove and place on a slice of bread spread with horseradish. Cover with another slice of bread. Continue with the remaining ingredients to make 4 sandwiches.

Island Club Sandwich

SERVES 2

This little outdoor café is a surprise, hidden off the boulevard in Key West and adjacent to the Inn at Key West. You have to know it's there. The small sign on the boulevard is easy to miss. It's secluded, facing the largest freshwater lagoon-style pool in Key West. Partners Linda Sorensen and Allan Merrill, after many years of operating successful restaurants, decided to take over this little café and slow down a little. It's open for breakfast and lunch. Their Island Club Sandwich is very popular with the locals. Linda says that fresh tarragon provides the magic of the chicken salad in the sandwich. They serve the sandwich with mesclun salad.

● ●

    1/2 pound boneless, skinless chicken breast
    Olive oil spray
    1/4 cup diced celery
    2 tablespoons diced onion
    1/2 cup mayonnaise
    2 tablespoons chopped fresh tarragon
    Salt and freshly ground black pepper to taste
    1 8-ounce can crushed pineapple, well drained
    5 ounces cream cheese
    6 slices whole-wheat bread, toasted
    Several leafy green lettuce leaves

Heat a nonstick skillet over medium-high heat. Spray the chicken with olive oil spray. Grill or sauté for 5 minutes per side. A meat thermometer should read 165°F. Chop the chicken in a food processor or by hand. Add the celery, onion, mayonnaise, tarragon, and salt and pepper to taste.

Mix the pineapple and cream cheese together.

To assemble, spread the cream cheese mixture on 2 slices of bread. Place a slice of bread over each. Place the lettuce over the bread and divide the chicken salad between the two sandwiches. Top with the remaining bread. Cut in half and serve.

Midway Special Turkey Club Sandwich with Flash-Roasted Pita Chips

SERVES 4

Halfway between Miami and Key West at MM 80, this funky little café is open for breakfast and lunch. Bob McGlasson was remodeling the café for a friend when he noticed that about ten feet of the building was missing. He found a closed-off bathroom with a time capsule — papers stowed away in an old fruit crate. It had the history of the little shack. He became so fascinated with his find that he and his wife, Lyndsey, decided to take over the building and build the café.

His Midway Special is a special treat. The secret is his Midway Sauce. He makes his own bread, topping it with olive oil, parsley, and kosher salt.

I've adapted his recipe for the sandwich using bought focaccia.

• •

Midway Sauce

1/4 cup spicy brown mustard
1/4 cup yellow mustard
1/2 cup mayonnaise
2 tablespoons key lime juice
2 tablespoons honey

Blend all the ingredients to a smooth consistency.

Turkey Club Sandwich

2 loaves focaccia bread, about 12 inches long each
1 cup Midway Sauce
2 cups thinly sliced cucumber
2 cups thinly sliced tomato
1 pound sliced turkey breast
8 slices Havarti cheese
Several lettuce leaves
4 tablespoons olive oil
2 tablespoons chopped fresh or dried parsley
2 teaspoons kosher salt

Preheat the oven to 350°F. Cut both breads in half crosswise and then in half lengthwise, to open for sandwiches. Spread 2 tablespoons Midway Sauce over each bottom slice of bread. Place the cucumbers on the sauce and the tomatoes over the cucumber. Place the turkey over the tomatoes and then add the cheese slices. Place a layer of lettuce over the cheese. Spread the remaining 2 tablespoons sauce on the top slices of bread and close the sandwiches. Brush the top of each sandwich with the olive oil. Sprinkle the tops with the parsley and salt. Place in the oven for 5 minutes to slightly melt the cheese. Serve with dill pickle and Flash-Roasted Pita Chips.

Flash-Roasted Pita Chips

2 pocket pita breads
Canola oil spray
Garlic powder for sprinkling, about 1/2 tablespoon
Kosher salt

Preheat the oven to 450°F. Cut the breads in half and spray both sides of each half with canola oil spray. Sprinkle with garlic powder and salt. Cut each half into triangles. Place on a baking sheet and bake for 5 minutes or until golden and crisp. Serve with the remaining Midway Sauce for dipping.

Spinach-and-Artichoke Stuffed Tomatoes with Goat Cheese

SERVES 4

The Key Largo Cook-off takes place each year in November. It's open to amateurs, professionals, and "junior" chefs. Page Prouty has won either best in show or runner-up several times. She tells me she never cooked until she got married and realized she had better learn. Here's her winning stuffed tomato recipe.

2 tablespoons butter, divided use
3 tablespoons chopped shallots
1 garlic clove, crushed
8 cups fresh spinach, washed
1/4 cup dry white wine
1 cup canned artichoke hearts, drained
4 large tomatoes
4 tablespoons goat cheese

Preheat the oven to 350°F. Heat 1 tablespoon butter in a large skillet over medium-high heat. Add the shallots and garlic. Sauté until soft, about 2 minutes. Add the spinach and white wine. Let the spinach cook down. Add the artichokes and remaining 1 tablespoon butter. Add salt and pepper to taste. Cook until the mixture is dry.

Cut a small slice off the bottom (nonstem end) of the tomatoes so they will stand without rolling over. Slice off the stem end and scoop out the inside flesh. Place the tomatoes in a baking pan just large enough to hold them. Fill the tomatoes with the stuffing. Spoon the cheese on top of the stuffing. Cover with foil and bake for 35 to 40 minutes.

Parsnip Puree

SERVES 4

Stuart Kemp, chef/owner of 915 Duvall Street, serves this puree in the winter with his Key West Snapper (p.131). It's great as a side dish for meat or fish.

This recipe calls for pomegranate molasses. It can be found in some specialty food stores. Kemp suggests using reduced balsamic vinegar as a substitute. Reduce the vinegar by one-half.

• •

1 pound parsnips, peeled and cut into large slices
1/2 cup pomegranate molasses
Salt and freshly ground black pepper to taste

Place the parsnips in a saucepan of boiling water. Boil for 15 minutes or until the parsnips are soft. Drain and mash the parsnips with a fork. Add the pomegranate molasses and salt and pepper to taste.

Sweet Potato Pie

SERVES 8

At one time, various churches in Key West made food to sell to raise money. These dishes were homemade, using fresh ingredients, and were absolutely delicious. Unfortunately, that generation of parishioners no longer cooks for the churches. But here is one of their specialties.

Several years ago, while in Key West, I met the ladies of the St. James Missionary Baptist Church on Olivia Street near the Hemingway House. Rattling pans, laughter, and talking drew me to the back of the church, where I found several ladies at work in the kitchen. "Just call us friends of the church," they told me. Having come to Key West in 1945 from the Carolinas, their cooking had a distinct Southern flavor. They were going to make their Sweet Potato Pie on Sunday to sell after church for Sunday lunch. It was worth the extra trip back to the church to pick up my fresh warm pie when it was ready.

• •

Short-Crust Pastry

1 1/3 cups all-purpose flour	2 tablespoons vegetable shortening
6 tablespoons butter	1/4 cup ice water

Place the flour in a bowl. Cut the butter and shortening into the flour, using a pastry blender or 2 knives, scissor-fashion, until the mixture resembles bread crumbs. Make a well in the center of the mixture and add 1 tablespoon water. Mix with a fork, adding more water to the drier areas as needed. When the mixture starts to come together in a ball, knead it lightly with your hands. Wrap in a plastic bag and place in the refrigerator to rest for at least 30 minutes. Roll out and line the pie plate.

Sweet Potato Pie

2 cups cooked sweet potatoes	1/4 teaspoon ground nutmeg
(about 1 1/4 pounds potatoes)	1/2 teaspoon ground cinnamon
2 tablespoons butter, softened	1 egg
1/4 cup sugar	1/4 cup milk

Preheat the oven to 400°F. Prepare the Short-Crust Pastry and line an 8- to 9-inch pie plate. Peel the potatoes and cut into cubes. Place in a pot of cold water, cover, and bring to a boil over high heat. Boil until soft, about 25 minutes. Drain, measure 2 cups of cubes, add the butter, and mash well. Let cool before adding the egg. Mix in the sugar, spices, egg, and milk. Spoon into the pie shell and bake for 45 minutes. The pastry should be light golden brown and the pie filling set. Slice and serve hot or cold. This dish freezes well.

Doc's Stuffed Shells

SERVES 4

D r. Jim Boilini's love of good food inspired him to help start the Key Largo Cook-off in 1981. It's become an annual event in Key Largo that brings the whole community together. He now owns Doc's Diner in Key Largo, where he serves his first love, Italian food, on Tuesdays. He gathers recipes on his many trips to Italy.

• •

24 jumbo pasta shells
3 cups ricotta cheese
2 tablespoons softened butter
2 tablespoons chopped fresh basil
1 teaspoon dried oregano
2 eggs
3 teaspoons freshly ground nutmeg
1 cup shredded Italian cheese (combination of Asiago,
    provolone, and mozzarella)
3/4 cup smoked provolone or mozzarella, shredded
1/4 cup finely ground pine nuts
2 tablespoons chopped onion
1 tablespoon butter
2 cups marinara sauce
1/2 cup white wine

Preheat the oven to 325°F. Place a large saucepan filled with water on to boil over high heat. When the water is boiling, add the shells and cook for 12 minutes, or until tender but firm. Drain and run cold water over them.

Mix the ricotta cheese, softened butter, basil, oregano, eggs, nutmeg, shredded Italian cheese, smoked cheese, pine nuts, and onion together. Butter an oven-proof pan just large enough to hold the shells in one layer. Spread 1 cup of the marinara sauce over the bottom of the pan. Fill the shells with the cheese mixture and line them up in the pan over the marinara sauce. Pour the white wine into the pan. Cover the pan with foil and bake in the oven for 40 minutes. Serve 6 shells per person and pass the remaining marinara sauce.

Key Lime Desserts

In addition to conch, key limes are the most recognized local ingredient of the Keys. At one time, these rugged little yellow limes grew in great abundance in the Keys. They have an interesting history (see glossary) and merit a section all their own.

Key lime pie is truly a regional, American dessert. In the days before refrigeration, canned milk was the only milk available. It was natural to put sweetened condensed milk together with native key limes to make a key lime pie. It is on most menus throughout the Keys. I particularly like Hawks Cay Resort's Key Lime Pie. For this pie, the egg yolks are whipped up to make it very light. I also created a Key Lime Cream Pie for this book. Savor its smooth, rich texture and flavor.

On a summer day in the Keys, I stopped at Mrs. Mac's Kitchen and discovered their Key Lime Freeze. It is a refreshing drink and a great ending to a lunch or dinner. Chocolate and key lime go well together. My Key Lime Chocolate Chip Ice Cream transforms bought vanilla ice cream into a quick tangy dessert. Serve it with my rich Key Lime Fudge Sauce and discover how the sweet chocolate and tart key lime in the ice cream make perfect partners.

There are no commercial key lime groves in the Keys today. The key limes grown there are in backyards and are mostly consumed in the Keys. Most of the key limes in our markets come from Mexico and other parts of South America. Bottled key lime juice works perfectly in these recipes.

Key Lime Cake

SERVES 8

There are many different key lime cakes available in the Keys. I created this one based on several I had tasted for my *Keys Cuisine* cookbook. One of my friends mentioned that it's so good I should include it in this new book. It's become one of my favorite cakes to make. It's a tangy cake rich in key lime flavor.

• •

Vegetable oil spray
1/2 cup unsalted butter (1 stick)
1 cup sugar
2 eggs
1 3/4 cups all-purpose flour
2 teaspoons baking powder
1/2 teaspoon salt
2/3 cup heavy cream
Zest from 1 key lime (if using bottled key lime juice,
    zest a regular lime)
1 tablespoon plus 1/2 cup key lime juice
1 cup confectioners' sugar, plus more for sprinkling
6-cup Bundt pan or 8-inch square cake pan,
    2-inches deep

Grease the Bundt pan with vegetable oil spray. Preheat the oven to 350°F. Cream the butter in an electric mixer until smooth. Gradually add the sugar, beating until light and fluffy. Add the eggs, one at a time, and continue to beat. Sift the flour, baking powder, and salt together. Alternately add the flour and cream into the batter, starting and ending with the flour. Mix in the key lime zest and 1 tablespoon juice. Spoon the batter into the prepared pan and bake for 20 minutes. Cover the top loosely with a piece of foil to prevent burning and continue to bake for another 20 minutes. The cake is done when a knife or cake tester inserted in the center comes out clean and the cake starts to pull away from the sides. Remove from the oven and let stand for 10 minutes. Turn out onto a cake rack to cool.

    While the cake bakes, prepare the glaze. Pour 1/2 cup key lime juice into a medium-size bowl. Add the confectioners' sugar and whisk until smooth. Place a dinner plate under the cake rack. While the cake is still warm, slowly spoon the glaze over the top of the cake so that all of the liquid is absorbed. The plate will catch any glaze that runs off. Continue to reapply these drippings until all of the glaze is absorbed. Just before serving, sprinkle the cake with additional confectioners' sugar.

Key Lime Chocolate Chip Ice Cream

SERVES 8 TO 10

Chocolate and key lime juice complement each other. Here's a quick and easy dessert that requires the best-quality vanilla ice cream. Serve it with Key Lime Fudge Sauce (p. 211) for a special treat.

• •

1 quart vanilla ice cream
6 tablespoons key lime juice
3/4 cup chocolate chips

Let the ice cream stand at room temperature for about 5 minutes to soften. Place in the bowl of a food processor or electric mixer. Mix until the ice cream is the consistency of thick whipped cream. Mix in the key lime juice. Remove from the food processor and fold in the chocolate chips. Place in a freezer-safe container and freeze. Let rest in the freezer overnight or for at least 8 hours.

Key Lime Fudge Sauce

MAKES ABOUT 1 1/4 CUPS

The tart key lime juice complements the sweet richness of the dark chocolate to make an exciting hot fudge sauce. Serve it warm over ice cream, cake or fruit or use it as a dipping sauce. The sauce will keep a week in the refrigerator and can be frozen.

• •

1 2/3 cups sugar
1 5-ounce can evaporated milk
3 ounces semisweet chocolate
2 tablespoons butter
2 tablespoons key lime juice

Place the sugar and evaporated milk in a saucepan over medium heat. Stir until the sugar is dissolved. Do not let boil. Add the chocolate and butter and cook until the sauce is smooth, stirring constantly. Remove from the heat and stir in the key lime juice. Pour into a jar and cool. Refrigerate until needed. It will harden in the refrigerator.

Rewarm the sauce in a microwave oven on high for 1 minute. Stir and microwave for another minute. Or, place a saucepan filled with water over medium-high heat and add the jar. Spoon over ice cream, sorbet, or cake, or use as a dip for fruit.

Key Lime Cookies

MAKES 18 COOKIES

The tart key lime flavor goes perfectly with these cookies. I'm a confessed cookie monster and decided that Key Lime Cookies were a must for this chapter. Here's my recipe.

• •

1/2 cup butter (1 stick)
1/4 cup brown sugar
1 egg, separated
1 cup all-purpose flour
1 tablespoon key lime juice
1 cup chopped walnuts
1/2 cup bottled lemon curd
1 1/2 tablespoons key lime juice

Preheat the oven to 300°F. Cream the butter and sugar with an electric mixer until light and fluffy. Beat in the egg yolk. Lower the speed on the mixer and add the flour. Blend slightly and add the key lime juice. Form the batter into small balls, about 1/2 inch in diameter. Dip the balls in the egg white, then roll in the nuts. Place on an ungreased cookie sheet. Make a depression in the center of each cookie with a small melon scoop or teaspoon. Place in the oven for 8 minutes. Remove from the oven and press the centers again. Return to the oven and bake for 10 minutes. Mix the lemon curd and key lime juice together. Remove the cookies from the oven and cool slightly. Fill the centers with the key lime mixture. Cool on a rack. Store in an airtight container. Can be frozen.

Tom's Harbor House Key Lime Pie

SERVES 8 TO 10

Key lime pie is without question the most famous Keys dish appearing on menus throughout the world. Key limes, sweetened condensed milk, and eggs are the main ingredients, but there are many different versions. Chef Charlotte Miller from Tom's Harbor House at Hawks Cay Resort on Duck Key makes one that has become a favorite of mine. Her secret is to whip the egg yolks until they are fluffy and almost white. It makes for a light pie. Also, she adds lime zest to the key lime filling for added lime flavor and crunch. She also told me she adds a little flour to the graham cracker crust. The flour helps the crust hold together better when it is cut.

1 cup graham cracker crumbs
1 1/2 tablespoons sugar
1 1/2 tablespoons flour
4 tablespoons butter
8 egg yolks
1/2 cup sweetened condensed milk
1 cup key lime juice
Zest from 2 limes (regular limes are fine)

Preheat the oven to 325°F. Mix the graham cracker crumbs, sugar, and flour together. Melt the butter and add to the graham crackers. Stir to make sure all the ingredients are combined. Press the mixture into a 9- or 10-inch pie plate. Set aside.

Using an electric beater, beat the egg yolks until they are light, about 3 minutes. With the beater running, slowly drizzle in the condensed milk. In a steady stream, add the lime juice and then the lime zest. Pour into the prepared pie shell. Bake for 20 minutes. Remove from the oven and cool for 10 minutes. Refrigerate until needed. Can be frozen for up to 1 month.

Key Lime Cream Pie

SERVES 8 TO 10

I think there are almost as many key lime pie recipes as there are inhabitants of the Keys. They all start with juice from the unique key lime, which has a distinctive flavor that is more tart than traditional Persian limes. As I thought about the desserts for this book, I decided to try a pie based on crème patissiere, or pastry cream. The result was an instant success. The delicious custard easily takes on the special key lime flavor. The pastry cream gives the pie a more velvety texture with a delicious balance of sweet and tart. Try it and surprise your guests with this variation on the theme of a traditional key lime pie.

. . . .

Graham Cracker Crust

1 1/2 cups graham cracker crumbs
1/4 cup packed brown sugar
6 tablespoons unsalted butter (3/4 stick), melted

Place the graham cracker crumbs and sugar in a bowl. Stir the melted butter into the crumbs and press the mixture into a 9- or 10-inch pie plate. Place in the refrigerator until needed.

Filling

3 egg yolks
1/2 cup sugar
1/4 cup cornstarch
1 1/2 cups milk
1 teaspoon vanilla extract
2 teaspoons butter
1 1/2 cups sweetened condensed milk
1/2 cup key lime juice

Beat the egg yolks with an electric mixer and slowly add the sugar. Continue to beat until the mixture is almost white and begins to form ribbons. Lift the beaters and form a W. If this remains, the ribbon stage has been reached. Beat in the cornstarch. With the mixer running, slowly pour in the milk and vanilla. Pour the mixture into a saucepan and place over medium heat, stirring constantly. The sauce will become lumpy as it comes to a boil. Continue whisking to eliminate any lumps. When a bubble forms, the flour is cooked. Remove from the heat. Whisk in the butter until it is melted.

Mix the sweetened condensed milk with the key lime juice. Stir into the sauce. Pour into the prepared pie crust. Place in the refrigerator for at least 1 hour before serving.

Key Lime Squares

MAKES ABOUT 20 SQUARES

When Bill Gaiser from Key West's Carriage Trade Garden served these squares, he called them little yellow brownies. Bill is retired now, but his recipe lives on and for good reason.

• •

Vegetable oil spray
3 ounces blanched almonds
1 cup unsalted butter (2 sticks)
2 1/4 cups all-purpose flour
1 tablespoon plus 1/4 cup confectioners' sugar
5 eggs
2 cups sugar
3/4 cup key lime juice
8 x 12-inch baking pan

Preheat the oven to 350°F. Grease the baking pan with vegetable oil spray.

Chop the almonds in a food processor and add the butter, flour, and 1 table-spoon confectioners' sugar. Blend to a dough consistency. Pat into the baking pan and bake for 15 minutes.

Meanwhile, gently mix the eggs, sugar, and key lime juice together, being careful not to let the mixture foam. Remove the baking pan from the oven and reduce the oven temperature to 325°F. Pour the lime juice mixture over the partially baked crust and return to the oven. Bake until set, about 20 to 30 minutes. Check that the topping is firm. If it isn't, turn off the oven and leave the pan in the warm oven until the topping firms. Remove from the oven and cool. Cut into squares. Sprinkle 1/4 cup confectioners' sugar over the squares just before serving.

Mrs. Mac's Key Lime Freeze

SERVES 1

The sign on the wall at Mrs. Mac's Kitchen in Key Largo reads: "Home of the Key Lime Freeze." I watched Angie Wittke make this refreshing drink and after tasting it decided the sign should read "home of the *famous* key lime freeze." It's the perfect treat on a warm day.

• •

3 tablespoons key lime juice
3/4 cup lemon and lime soda
2 scoops frozen soft-serve vanilla yogurt or
    vanilla ice cream

Place ingredients in a blender and blend until smooth, about 30 seconds. Pour into a tall glass.

Key Lime Parfait

SERVES 4

There is an intriguing contrast of sweet and tart flavors in this parfait that results from layering the sweet crunchy graham cracker–walnut mixture, the smooth whipped cream, and lime-infused condensed milk. It makes a pretty party dish served in a tall glass or glass bowl and can be made a day ahead and stored in the refrigerator.

· ·

1 1/2 cups graham cracker crumbs
1/4 cup brown sugar
3/4 cup chopped walnuts, plus 2 tablespoons, divided use
4 tablespoons butter, melted
1 cup heavy whipping cream
2 cups sweetened condensed milk
3/4 cup key lime juice
4 10-ounce parfait glasses or other attractive tall glasses

Place the graham cracker crumbs in a bowl and add the brown sugar and 1/2 cup walnuts. Stir in the melted butter. Set aside.

Whip the cream until stiff in a second bowl. Combine the condensed milk and key lime juice in another bowl and fold into the whipped cream.

Spoon 1/4 of the graham cracker mixture into the bottom of each glass. Spoon 1/4 of the key lime mixture over the graham cracker mixture. Continue to layer the mixtures, ending with the key lime mixture on top. Sprinkle the top with the remaining walnuts.

Alma's Key Lime Mango Parfait

SERVES 4

Chef Tony Glitz from Alma Restaurant at Hawks Cay Resort created this recipe for people who asked for a lighter dessert. The sweet mango sauce and tart key lime cream create a tantalizing contrast. The parfait can be made a day ahead and is very attractive served in a martini glass.

· ·

1 cup mango puree*
1 cup sugar plus 2 tablespoons, divided use
1 cup heavy cream
1 cup whipped topping such as Cool Whip
1/2 cup key lime juice
3 teaspoons lime zest

Heat the mango puree and 1 cup sugar in a saucepan over medium heat. Bring to a simmer and cook for 4 to 5 minutes. Watch during this time to make sure the sugar dissolves and doesn't burn. Set aside to cool.

Whip the heavy cream and whipped topping to reach soft peaks. Add the key lime juice and 2 remaining tablespoons sugar and whip to soft peaks.

Spoon 1 tablespoon mango sauce into each of four martini glasses to form one layer. Spoon half the cream mixture over the mango puree for the second layer. Spoon the remaining mango sauce over the cream mixture and finish the last layer with the cream mixture. Sprinkle the lime zest on top.

* Pineapple puree can be substituted if mango puree is not available.

Other Keys Desserts

Tropical fruits play an important part in Keys desserts. Mangoes, coconut, bananas, strawberries, and guavas are all readily available. The Fish House Coconut Ice Cream has a rich flavor and creamy texture. Sarabeth's Key West Strawberry Shortcake is a melt-in-your-mouth delight. From May to August, ripe, juicy mangoes hang lusciously from the trees, just waiting to be picked. Hawks Cay Resort's Alma Restaurant's Mango Bread Pudding is delectable and easy to make.

Other flavors create mouth-watering desserts. If chocolate is your favorite, On the Bricks's Triple Chocolate Banana Brownie or Louie's Backyard Chocolate Brownie Crème Brûlée is for you. Try Hawks Cay's Dulce de Leche Cheesecake. Dulce de leche is a caramel-flavored sauce made from sweetened condensed milk.

This section also has a collection of breads that are easy to make. Pineapple Coconut Walnut Bread, Banana Bread, Mango Bread, and Avocado Bread will tempt even nonbread bakers to try them.

My popularity at the Miami Herald photography studio and my WLRN National Public Radio station grew as they joined me in taste-testing these desserts. These recipes are full of flavor and fun.

Pepe's Coconut Cream Pie

SERVES 6 TO 8

Pepe's claims to be the oldest eating house in the Florida Keys. It was established in 1909. It's an old-time restaurant located on the old commercial waterfront of Caroline Street in Key West. A large tree shades the entire patio where many tables are set. Locals often come with their pet parrots, macaws, and lap dogs. Charlie makes their homemade desserts.

• •

Graham Cracker Crust

1 1/2 cups graham cracker crumbs
1/4 cup sugar
6 tablespoons melted butter (3/4 stick)

Place the graham cracker crumbs and sugar in a bowl. Stir the melted butter into the crumbs and press the mixture into a 9- or 10-inch pie plate. Set aside.

Filling

3 egg yolks
1 teaspoon coconut extract
1/2 cup sugar
3 heaping tablespoons cornstarch
3 cups half-and-half
1 cup flaked and sweetened coconut
1/2 cup heavy cream

Mix the egg yolks and coconut extract together and set aside.

Combine the sugar, cornstarch and half-and-half in a heavy saucepan over medium-high heat. Bring to a boil, stirring constantly.

When the mixture starts to bubble, add 1/2 cup of the mixture to the eggs very slowly to warm them. Return all of the egg mixture to the saucepan, whisking constantly over medium-low heat, and continue cooking. When the sauce is thick and coats the back of a spoon, remove from the heat and stir in the coconut. Cool to room temperature and turn into the graham cracker pie crust. Chill for at least 2 hours. To serve, whip the cream and spoon over the pie.

Bobbie Sawyer's Natilla

SERVES 8 TO 10

"This dessert takes ten minutes to make and ten minutes to eat," Bobbie Sawyer told me when I interviewed her for my *Keys Cuisine* cookbook. The dessert has stood the test of time. I find myself making it to go with fruit or as a sauce for cakes or to serve just as a pudding. The recipe was handed down from Bobbie's grandparents who came to Key West in the late 1800s. She remembered her mother and grandmother making it and putting a piece of lime peel in the pudding to give it extra flavor; the child who found it got a quarter, which was big money in those days. The lack of readily available fresh milk meant that the people of her grandparents' generation had to create dishes using canned milk. Natilla is a light, smooth dessert.

• •

1 14-ounce can sweetened condensed milk
14 ounces water (1 condensed milk canful)
    plus 3 tablespoons, divided use
1 13-ounce can evaporated milk
3 egg yolks
3 rounded tablespoons cornstarch
3 tablespoons water
2 1/2 teaspoons vanilla extract
2 tablespoons unsalted butter
Ground cinnamon

Combine the condensed milk, 14 ounces water, evaporated milk, and egg yolks in a saucepan. Mix the cornstarch with 3 tablespoons water in a cup to form a smooth paste and add to the mixture. Bring to a boil over medium-high heat, whisking constantly. Cook until the mixture begins to thicken and is difficult to stir. Remove from the heat and stir in the vanilla and butter. Pour into small cups, ramekins, or a soufflé dish. Sprinkle with cinnamon and refrigerate until ready to serve. Bring to room temperature before serving.

Banana Wontons with Chili Chocolate Cream Sauce

SERVES 4

L ittle Palm Island at MM 28.5 is an island paradise resort filled with palm trees and exotic flowers. You reach the island by their private launch. There are no phones or TVs in the rooms. It's a place to relax, enjoy the water sports, and indulge in their excellent cuisine. Here is one of Chef Luis Pous's favorite desserts.

The Chili Chocolate Cream Sauce would also taste great served over ice cream, cake, or fruit.

● ●

Banana Wontons

3 ripe bananas
1/4 cup macadamia nuts, chopped
1/4 cup dark chocolate chips
16 large wonton skins

Oil for frying
2 teaspoons ground cinnamon
1 tablespoon confectioners' sugar
1/4 cup thinly sliced crystallized ginger

Mash the bananas in a bowl and add the macadamia nuts and 1/4 cup dark chocolate chips. Place 8 wonton skins on a countertop and place a spoonful of banana mixture in the center of each. Brush a little water around the edge of each skin. Place the remaining 8 skins on top. Seal the wontons by pressing a fork around the edges.

Heat the oil in a deep fryer or large saucepan over high heat to 365ºF. Fry the wontons until they are just golden, about 30 seconds to 1 minute. Remove to a plate lined with paper towels. Sprinkle the wontons with the cinnamon and then the confectioners' sugar. Serve 2 wontons per person on a dessert plate. Place a small bowl of Chili Chocolate Cream Sauce on each plate for dipping. Arrange the crystallized ginger as a garnish on each plate.

Chili Chocolate Cream Sauce

1 cup cream
1 ancho (dried poblano) chili
2 cups dark chocolate chips

Heat the cream with the ancho chili in a saucepan for 2 to 3 minutes. Remove the chili and add the 2 cups chocolate chips. Stir over low heat to melt the chocolate. Pour the sauce into 4 small bowls or dipping pots.

Blueberry Pecan Crunch

SERVES 6 TO 8

Laura Dreaver at The Key Largo Conch House makes the desserts for her family restaurant. While talking with Laura, her son came over to say, "Don't forget the Blueberry Pecan Crunch. It's my favorite." It turns out that it is also her number one–selling dessert. She makes it with either fresh or frozen blueberries depending on the season.

• •

Vegetable oil spray
1 8-ounce can crushed pineapple, drained
    (about 1 rounded cup)
4 cups yellow cake mix
2 1/2 cups blueberries
2 tablespoons sugar
1/2 cup coarsely chopped pecans
4 tablespoons butter, melted

Preheat the oven to 350°F. Grease an 8 x 8-inch baking pan with vegetable oil spray. Spoon the crushed pineapple over the bottom of the pan. Spread the cake mix over the pineapple. Place the blueberries over the cake mix. Sprinkle the sugar and pecans over the blueberries. Drizzle the melted butter over the ingredients. Bake for 1 hour. Remove and cool for 30 minutes before cutting into squares.

Louie's Backyard Chocolate Brownie Crème Brûlée

SERVES 4

Louie's Backyard sits almost at the southernmost point of the United States. It is a treasure loved by both locals and visitors. Chef Doug Shook creates the excellent cuisine and atmosphere. With a twinkle in his eye he said, "You have to try my Chocolate Brownie Crème Brûlée." I did and here's the recipe. Placing a brownie in the center of the crème brûlée adds just the right texture and flavor to make this a dish with a surprise.

• •

Chocolate Brownies

Vegetable oil spray
Flour to dust pan
8-inch square baking pan
4 1/2 ounces dark chocolate, chopped
6 tablespoons butter
1/2 cup plus 2 tablespoons sugar
1/2 teaspoon vanilla extract
1/2 teaspoon salt
2 large eggs
1/4 cup flour
3/4 cup chopped pecans (optional)

Preheat the oven to 350°F. Grease the pan with vegetable oil spray and dust with flour. Melt the chocolate and butter in a bowl set over a pan of simmering water, stirring to combine them well. Remove from the heat and whisk in the sugar, followed by the vanilla, salt, eggs (one at a time), and the flour. Stir in the nuts. Spread the mixture evenly in the baking pan. Bake for 40 minutes until the edges of the cake pull away slightly from the sides of the pan and the center is just firm. Do not overbake. Makes 16 2-inch brownies.

Louie's Backyard Chocolate Brownie Crème Brûlée

1 3/4 cups heavy cream
1/2 vanilla bean, split
5 extra large egg yolks
1/2 cup sugar
4 2-inch brownies
6 tablespoons sugar for topping

Preheat the oven to 325°F. Combine the cream and vanilla bean in a saucepan and bring to a simmer over medium-high heat. Set aside. Beat the egg yolks lightly with 1/2 cup sugar in a mixing bowl. Slowly pour the scalded cream into the egg yolk mixture, whisking constantly, and then pour the custard back into the saucepan and return it to the stove. Cook the custard over low heat, stirring constantly, until it thickens enough to coat the back of a spoon. Don't let the custard boil. Immediately strain the custard through a fine mesh sieve into a bowl. Push a brownie into the bottom of each of 4 6-ounce custard cups. Fill the cups with the custard to within 1/2 inch of the top . Place the cups in a baking pan and add hot water to reach halfway up the sides of the cups. Bake in the oven for 30 to 40 minutes or until the custard is just set. Remove from the oven and chill thoroughly in the refrigerator.

To serve, sprinkle 1 1/2 tablespoons sugar over the surface of each custard in an even layer. Aim the flame of a propane or butane torch directly at the sugar until it melts, bubbles, and caramelizes. You can also place the crème brûlée in a roasting pan with water and caramelize the sugar under a broiler. Watch carefully. Serve at once.

Coconut Ice Cream

SERVES 4 TO 6

The Fish House in Islamorada considers its staff to be family. Jose A. Ornelas, their general manager, has been there for twenty years. He gave me his favorite ice-cream recipe. It's so easy and delicious we licked the bowl.

• •

2 cups heavy cream
6 ounces canned coconut milk
1 tablespoon coconut extract
1/2 cup sweetened condensed milk

Mix the ingredients together until smooth. Pour into an ice-cream maker and process. Place in a container and let mature for at least 1 hour in the freezer.

If you don't have an ice-cream maker, pour the mixture into a large roasting pan and freeze. Remove from the freezer after 1 hour and whisk. Continue to do this every 30 minutes until the ice cream thickens. Then place it in a container to mature in the freezer.

Nutty Drunken Ice Cream

SERVES 4

John Malocsay, chef/owner of Bentley's Restaurant in Islamorada, said I had to try his special dessert, Nutty Drunken Ice Cream. With a name like that, who could refuse? I tried it and it was worth every calorie.

He makes it with eight different kinds of nuts. Mix and match the nuts as you like. By the way, the glaze is great over cooked sweet potatoes.

. . . .

Glaze

1 pound butter
3 tablespoons sugar
1/2 cup dark brown sugar
1/2 teaspoon cinnamon
3/4 cup dark rum

Melt the butter in a large skillet over medium heat. Add the sugar and brown sugar. Dissolve the sugar in the butter until the butter has no sugar crystals, about 3 to 5 minutes. Raise the heat to medium-high and cook until the sauce starts to thicken. Add the cinnamon and rum. Cook until the sauce thickens again, about 10 minutes. The sauce should coat the back of a spoon. Cool for about 5 minutes before spooning over the ice cream.

Nut-Encrusted Ice Cream

3 tablespoons macadamia nuts
3 tablespoons walnuts
3 tablespoons pistachio nuts
3 tablespoons peanuts
3 tablespoons pecans
3 tablespoons hazelnuts
3 tablespoons almonds
1 tablespoon cashew nuts
4 large scoops vanilla ice cream

Coarsely chop the nuts together in a food processor or by hand and place on a large plate. Roll each scoop of ice cream in the nuts. Place each scoop in a small bowl and spoon the sauce over top.

White Chocolate Macadamia Nut Pie

SERVES 8 TO 10

One bite of this decadent pie and I immediately asked Chef Michael Ledwith from Kaiyo Restaurant in Islamorada for the recipe. From the moment you walk over the little bridge nestled in the Japanese garden you are transported into a Florida-Asian oasis.

The pie is easy to make. Use the pie crust recipe here or use a ready-made crust from the market. The filling is the star here.

• •

1 9-inch pie shell
1 cup lightly toasted macadamia nuts
3 eggs
1/4 cup light brown sugar
1/2 cup light corn syrup
1/2 teaspoon good vanilla
1/4 cup melted butter
1 pinch kosher salt
6 ounces white chocolate
1/2 cup plus 2 tablespoons heavy whipping cream,
     divided use
3 tablespoons almond-flavored liqueur
2 tablespoons semi-sweet chocolate chips

Preheat the oven to 375°F. Line a 9- or 10-inch pie plate with short-crust pastry. Place the nuts on a baking tray and toast in the oven or toaster oven for about 3 to 4 minutes. They should be golden, not brown. Mix the eggs, brown sugar, corn syrup, vanilla, melted butter, salt, and toasted macadamia nuts together. Pour into the pie shell. Bake for 30 minutes. Cover the top of the pie with foil to keep the top from becoming too brown. Continue to bake for 15 to 20 minutes. The filling should be set. Remove and cool.

Place the white chocolate and 1/2 cup heavy cream in a microwave-safe bowl. Microwave for 2 minutes on high. Stir and microwave for 1 minute to form a creamy sauce. Remove and stir in the almond-flavored liqueur. When the pie has cooled, pour the white chocolate sauce over the top to form a layer.

Place the semisweet chocolate chips and remaining 2 tablespoons cream in a microwave-safe bowl. Microwave for 30 seconds on high. Stir and drizzle over the top of the pie. Refrigerate overnight before serving.

Short-Crust Pastry

1 1/2 cups all-purpose flour
1 teaspoon salt (optional)
6 tablespoons butter
2 tablespoons vegetable shortening
1/4 cup ice water

Sift the flour and salt together into a bowl. Cut the butter and shortening into the flour by using a pastry blender or 2 knives, scissor-fashion, until the mixture resembles bread crumbs. Make a well in the center of the mixture and add 1 tablespoon water. Mix with a fork, adding more water to the drier areas as needed. When the mixture starts to come together in a ball, knead it lightly with your hands. Wrap in a plastic bag and place in the refrigerator to rest for at least 30 minutes. Roll out and place in a pie plate. This quantity will fill a 9- to 10-inch pie plate.

Mango Bread Pudding

SERVES 6

Chef Tony Glitz, executive chef from Alma Restaurant at Hawks Cay Resort on Duck Key, serves this mango bread pudding with homemade ice cream. It's perfect just warm out of the oven and keeps well for several days in the refrigerator. If refrigerated, bring to room temperature before serving. He uses his homemade Mango Bread (p. 244).

An egg-based bread such as brioche can be used instead of mango bread.

• •

Vegetable oil spray
3 1/2 cups Mango Bread cubes (1- to 1 1/2-inch cubes)
4 eggs
1/2 cup sugar
1 cup heavy cream
1/3 cup mango puree
1/2 cup coconut rum

Preheat the oven to 325°F. Grease a deep-dish baking pan* (9 inches in diameter, 2 inches deep) with vegetable oil spray.

Place the bread cubes in the pan. Mix the eggs and sugar together. Add the cream, mango puree, and rum. Mix well. Pour over the bread cubes. Let soak for 10 minutes. Mix again. Bake for 45 minutes. Place foil over the top of the pan to keep the crust from becoming too dark. Bake for another 15 minutes. A cake tester or toothpick should come out clean.

* Any type of baking pan can be used. The ingredients should fill only 3/4 of the pan.

Dulce de Leche Cheesecake

SERVES 10 TO 12

Mention dulce de leche to anyone from South America and they smile and their eyes light up. It's a delicious, caramel-flavored sauce made by slowly heating sweetened condensed milk until it becomes thick and takes on a caramel color. Dulce de leche can be found in jars and cans ready-made in many markets. When Chef Tony Glitz from Hawks Cay Resort on Duck Key mentioned a cheesecake made with it, my eyes lit up, too. This dessert reflects the Latin influence in the Keys and makes a wonderful party dish.

• •

1 cup graham cracker crumbs
1 1/2 tablespoons sugar
1 1/2 tablespoons flour
2 tablespoons butter
False-bottom cake pan about 8 inches in diameter and
　　2 1/2 inches deep
1 1/4 pounds cream cheese
1 cup sugar
2 tablespoons cornstarch
1 cup sour cream
4 large eggs
1 teaspoon vanilla
6 tablespoons dulce de leche
6 tablespoons heavy cream

Preheat the oven to 300°F. Mix the graham cracker crumbs, sugar, and flour together in a bowl. Melt the butter and stir into the graham cracker mixture, making sure all the ingredients are combined. Press into the bottom of the cake pan.

In an electric mixer, cream the cream cheese, sugar, and cornstarch together until they are smooth. Add the sour cream and blend in. Add the eggs and vanilla and mix thoroughly. Mix the dulce de leche and cream together in a food processor until smooth. Add 2 tablespoons of the dulce de leche mixture to the cream cheese. Blend in. Pour the batter into the prepared cake pan. Swirl the remaining dulce de leche into the cake by dropping spoonfuls onto the cake and cutting it into the batter in a swirling motion with a knife or skewer. Place the cake pan in a roasting pan and fill the pan with hot water about 3/4 up the side of the cake pan. Place in the oven. Bake for 1 hour. Cover the cake pan with foil to prevent the top of the cake from becoming brown. Bake for 1 hour more or until the cake is firm on top.

Guava Duff with Rum Butter Sauce

SERVES 4

Sheila Sands is a fifth-generation Conch. Her father and grandfather were sponge fishermen in Key West. Sheila is an event planner in Key West and uses many recipes and ideas from her childhood. She remembers the meals her mother made that were based on recipes from the Bahamas and reflected the considerable British influence there and in the Keys. Her favorite is Guava Duff. It's made by folding the fruit into dough and steaming or boiling it. It's served with rum sauce.

* *

1 fresh guava*
2 tablespoons butter
1/2 cup sugar
2 large eggs, beaten
1/4 teaspoon allspice
1 1/2 cups flour
1 teaspoon baking powder

Peel and core the guava. Cut out the seeds. Rub the guava through a sieve or place it in a food mill or food processor to obtain 1 cup guava pulp. Cream the butter with the sugar and add the eggs, guava pulp, and allspice. Beat until smooth. Sift the flour and baking powder together and add to the guava mixture. Mix into a dough. It will be stiff. Grease the top of a double boiler and add the dough. Place over the boiling water. Cover with a lid and steam for 3 hours. Turn out onto a cutting board and slice. Serve with Rum Butter Sauce.

Rum Butter Sauce

2 tablespoons butter
6 tablespoons sugar
1 egg, separated
1 tablespoon rum

Cream the butter and sugar together. Add the egg yolk and blend into the mixture. Add the rum and beat until smooth. Beat the egg white until stiff. Fold into the butter mixture. Serve over hot, sliced Guava Duff.

*Guavas are round or oval fruit about the size of a small orange. The fruit is usually cooked. It is processed into guava paste, guava juice, and guava jelly. It can be bitter or sweet depending on the variety.

Hot Banana Dessert

SERVES 2

My Key West friend Kitty Clements told me this was a dessert to die for — and she was right! It's served at one of Key West's only pubs, Finnegan's Wake. Chef/partner Wayne Keller gave me the secret to his recipe. It's a takeoff on bananas Foster. He makes it with a "buster-size" banana.

• •

Vegetable oil spray
2 tablespoons butter
2 tablespoons brown sugar
1 extra large banana, peeled
1 tablespoon butterscotch and vanilla schnapps
1 8-ounce sheet frozen puff pastry (about 9 x12-inch sheet)
1/2 cup whipping cream
Bottled chocolate syrup
Bottled butterscotch syrup

Preheat the oven to 475°F. Spray a baking tray with vegetable oil spray and set aside.

Melt the butter and sugar in a large skillet over medium heat until the sugar starts to caramelize. While the sugar and butter are cooking, add the banana and turn it over in the sauce. Add the schnapps and flambé.* Place the puff pastry on a countertop and place the banana in the middle. Pour the sauce from the skillet over the banana. Fold one side of the pastry to the middle of the banana. Fold the other side to meet in the middle. Crimp the ends of the pastry with a fork. Place on the prepared tray and bake for 8 to 10 minutes. The pastry should be golden. Remove to a serving platter.

While the pastry bakes, whip the cream. To serve, pipe or add dollops of cream to the top of the pastry. Decorate with swirls of chocolate and butterscotch syrup. Present to the table and slice in half.

*To flambé, let the schnapps heat for a few seconds. If using an electric stove, add a lighted match to the skillet. If using a gas stove, tip the pan so that the gas flame ignites the alcohol. Always have a lid nearby for safety.

Biscuit Strawberry Shortcake

SERVES 6

"Don't miss Sarabeth's mile-high strawberry shortcake," my friend mentioned. With that introduction, I set my sights on seeking out this dessert. David Case retired from working with Sarabeth Levine at her famous Sarabeth's Kitchen in New York City and moved to Key West. He didn't stay retired long, though, and opened Sarabeth's Key West. He's busier than ever. He likes this recipe because most strawberry shortbreads are spongy and made only once a year, "when premade cakes are stacked next to the strawberries." His is made with real biscuits and homemade strawberry sauce.

The recipe calls for round baking rings to bake the biscuits. They can be baked without the rings but will not be perfectly shaped.

• •

Biscuits

6 tablespoons unsalted butter
1 2/3 cups all-purpose flour
1 tablespoon baking powder
1/4 cup sugar
3/4 cup heavy cream
Zest of one small orange
Butter to grease rings and baking sheet
4 round baking rings
2 tablespoons sugar

Soften the butter and add to the flour, baking powder, and sugar. Slowly mix with a paddle in an electric mixer for 5 to 7 minutes. Add the heavy cream and orange zest and mix for 1 minute more, slowly. The mixture should pull away from the bowl. As soon as it is mixed, place the dough on a floured countertop and form into a ball. Flour a rolling pin and roll the dough to 1/2 inch thick. Use a round cutter, the same size as the rings they will be baked in, to form the biscuits. It is important to roll out the dough only once and cut the biscuits without rerolling the dough. Place the biscuits in the refrigerator for 1 hour. Preheat the oven to 300°F. Butter the rings. Place the rings with the biscuits inside on a buttered baking sheet. Sprinkle with 2 tablespoons sugar. Bake in the preheated oven for 20 minutes. The biscuits should be golden brown on top.

Strawberry Sauce

1 pint fresh strawberries (about 3 1/2 cups)
2 tablespoons sugar
2 teaspoons vanilla extract

Place the strawberries in a saucepan and add the sugar and vanilla. Simmer to dissolve the sugar and form a syrup consistency. Set aside.

Whipped Cream

1 cup very cold heavy whipping cream
1/2 tablespoon confectioners' sugar

Pour the cream into a very cold bowl. Using a cold whisk, whip the cream until stiff. Add the confectioners' sugar and continue to whip until stiff.

Strawberry Shortcake

18 to 24 unblemished, ripe strawberries, sliced
about 1/8 to 1/4 inch thick
Confectioners' sugar for garnish

Cut the biscuits in half horizontally and place the bottom halves on individual plates. Place a large spoonful of cream on each biscuit half. Add sliced strawberries to the cream, making sure the strawberries just cover the cream. Drizzle a spoonful of sauce over the strawberries and cream. Cover with the top half of the biscuit. Sprinkle confectioners' sugar on top.

Triple-Chocolate Banana Brownie

MAKES 10 TO 12 PIE-SHAPED SERVINGS

Hidden in the back of the Caribbean Village shops is a charming café on a brick patio called On the Bricks. Desiray Pruett spent summers in the Keys with her uncle. When she found this abandoned café, she immediately fell in love with it, bought it, renovated it herself, and opened On the Bricks. She makes everything on the menu herself. Her Triple-Chocolate Banana Brownie is scrumptious to the last bite.

She says it's important to use frozen banana and chocolate bars. Freeze the banana without the skin.

● ●

Vegetable oil spray
2 tablespoons cream cheese
2 large eggs
3 frozen chocolate bars broken into small pieces
      (Mars, Musketeers, or others)
1 cup chocolate chips
1/4 stick cinnamon, shaved
1 frozen banana, sliced
1/2 cup walnut oil
1/4 cup flour
10-inch round deep pie plate

Preheat the oven to 400°F. Grease the pie plate with vegetable oil spray. Blend the cream cheese and eggs in a mixer on high speed. Reduce the speed to low and add the chocolate bars, chocolate chips, cinnamon, and banana. Blend well. Add the oil and blend to incorporate. Add the flour and blend in. Spoon the batter into the prepared pie plate and bake for 30 minutes.

Coconut Macaroons

MAKES 16 COOKIES

A s I was leaving Debbiy Doo's Deli and Market in Islamorada, Debbiy stopped me and said, "You can't leave without one of my Coconut Macaroons." They were large, moist, and delicious.

• •

Vegetable oil spray
1/2 cup flour
4 cups shredded coconut
1/4 teaspoon salt
1 13 1/2-ounce can sweetened condensed milk
1 1/2 teaspoons vanilla extract

Preheat the oven to 350ºF. Grease a large cookie sheet with vegetable oil spray. Mix the flour, coconut, and salt in a bowl. Add the sweetened condensed milk and vanilla. Mix well. Drop 1/4 cup of batter onto the cookie sheet for each cookie. They should be 1 inch apart. Bake for 20 minutes until golden on top. Remove from the oven and place on a wire rack to cool.

Bob's Bunz Potato Chip Cookies

MAKES 22 COOKIES

As I was sitting in the Islamorada Bakery and Bob's Bunz restaurant, savoring their food and taking notes, a woman walked by and said, "Don't leave out Bob's Potato Chip Cookies." I'm glad I didn't. They're crunchy and delicious. Here's his recipe.

• •

Vegetable oil spray
1/2 pound butter (2 sticks)
1/2 cup sugar
1 3/4 cups flour
1/2 cup coarsely crushed potato chips
2 tablespoons chopped nuts (any type)
Confectioners' sugar for garnish

Preheat the oven to 350°F. Line a cookie sheet with parchment paper or grease the sheet and set aside. Cream the butter and sugar in a mixer on high speed until light and fluffy. Lower the speed to the lowest setting and add the flour, potato chips, and nuts. Blend about 2 minutes or until it comes together. Be careful not to over mix the batter. Drop large tablespoons of batter onto a greased cookie sheet about 2 inches apart. Place a piece of parchment paper or plastic wrap over the cookies and flatten until about 1/4-inch thick. Bake for 20 minutes. Cool and sprinkle confectioners' sugar on top.

Kitty's Zesty Lime Sugar Cookies

MAKES 28 TO 32 COOKIES

Kitty Clements is one of Key West's hostesses with the mostest. She opens her old town Key West home to many charity parties. The Easter Hat Party brings out many extraordinary hat creations. Her Zesty Lime Sugar Cookies are always a success.

Kitty says it's best to make these cookies on a cookie sheet lined with a Silpat (silicone) liner. You can also grease and flour the cookie sheet.

• •

1/4 pound butter or margarine (1 stick)
1 cup sugar
1 egg
1 cup all-purpose flour
4 tablespoons frozen limeade concentrate
Zest of one lime
1/2 teaspoon vanilla extract
Sugar to garnish

Preheat the oven to 350°F. Cream the butter and sugar with an electric mixer until light and fluffy. Add the egg and mix thoroughly. Reduce the mixer speed and add the flour, limeade, zest, and vanilla. Blend to a dough consistency. Using a teaspoon, place the cookie dough on a greased baking tray at least 2 inches apart. Bake for 14 minutes. The cookies will spread and have a light brown edge. Remove the tray from the oven and place on a rack. Sprinkle the cookies generously with sugar. If using a Silpat, remove it with the cookies to a cool countertop. Otherwise let the cookies cool on the baking tray for at least 3 to 4 minutes. Transfer the cookies to a rack and let cool completely. The cookies can be stored in an airtight container in the refrigerator or frozen.

Cole's Peace Mango Triangles

MAKES 24 TRIANGLES

Y ou can't go by Cole's Peace Artisan Bakery on Eaton Street in Key West without stopping in for a loaf of their delicious bread. The air outside the bakery is filled with the smell of their breads and pastries baking. Owned by Richard and Cathy Tallmadge, it's one of the few bakeries in Key West. When the original owner, Kurt Matarazzo, decided to close his bakery, the bakery staff asked Richard, owner of the nearby Restaurant Store, to buy it. Cathy and Richard took over the bakery and have kept the quality bread-making tradition alive in Key West. They were making Mango Triangles the day I stopped by. They were crunchy, packed with flavor, and best of all, not sugary sweet.

• •

Crust

1 1/2 cups flour
1/2 teaspoon salt
1/4 cup butter
1/4 cup Crisco
6 to 7 tablespoons chilled water

Place the flour, salt, butter, and Crisco in the bowl of a food processor. Process until the dough resembles small peas. Remove from the processor to a bowl and slowly add the water until the dough holds together and forms a ball. Chill while the remaining ingredients are prepared.

Filling

6 tablespoons butter, softened
1/2 cup light brown sugar
1/2 teaspoon ground ginger
1/4 teaspoon ground allspice
2 tablespoons flour
1/2 cup sliced almonds, toasted
2 cups dried mango, soaked in water for 2 hours, then patted dry*

Beat the butter, sugar, ginger, and allspice together until creamy. Mix in the flour. Add the almonds and mix into the flour; then add the mango and mix until combined. Set aside.

*If dried mango is not available, Cathy suggests dried pineapple or other dried fruits.

Crumble

1/2 cup flour
1 cup rolled oats
3/4 cup brown sugar
3/4 teaspoon cinnamon
1/2 cup butter

Mix the dry ingredients together. Cut in the butter with a knife or pastry cutter until the mixture is uniform.

Finish

12 x 8-inch baking pan with sides

Preheat the oven to 350°F. Remove the crust from the refrigerator and roll out to fit a baking pan with sides. Spread the filling evenly over the crust and press down firmly. Sprinkle the crumble evenly over the filling and pat gently. Place in the preheated oven for 20 minutes. Rotate the pan and bake for 20 minutes more. Remove from the oven and cool thoroughly. Cut into 12 pieces (approximately 3 inches by 4 inches). Cut each of the pieces diagonally into triangles.

Grandma Marge's Pineapple Coconut Walnut Bread

MAKES 10 TO 12 SLICES

When Debbiy Shonyo-Culebras decided to open a café, she remembered many of her grandma's recipes from her childhood and went looking for them. She was delighted when she found recipe books from her grandmother and great grandmother. This recipe was buried in the back of one of the books.

Vegetable oil spray
1 cup chopped fresh pineapple, well drained
1/4 cup olive oil
2 eggs
2 cups flour
1 tablespoon cinnamon
1 teaspoon baking soda
3/4 teaspoon salt
1/4 teaspoon baking powder
2/3 cup sugar
1/3 cup light brown sugar
1/3 cup shredded coconut
1/3 cup chopped walnuts
8 1/2 x 4 1/2-inch loaf pan (9 x 5-inch pan can be used)

Preheat the oven to 350°F. Grease a loaf pan with vegetable oil spray. Cut a piece of parchment paper to fit the bottom of the pan. Lay it in the bottom and spray with vegetable oil spray. Set aside.

Place the pineapple, olive oil, and eggs in the bowl of a mixer. Mix on medium to combine, about 2 minutes. Add the flour, cinnamon, baking soda, salt, baking powder, sugar, and brown sugar. Mix on low to form a dough. Add the coconut and walnuts and gently mix into the dough. Spoon the batter into the pan and bake for 1 1/4 hours. Remove from the oven and run a knife around the edge of the pan. Turn the bread out onto a cake rack to cool.

Bob's Bunz Banana Bread

MAKES 10 TO 12 SLICES

B ob's banana bread is moist and flavorful. Bob and his business partner, Gloria Teague, own and run the Islamorada Bakery and Bob's Bunz. It's always crowded and with good reason. It's a perfect place to stop for breakfast, lunch, or whenever you're hungry. Use this bread for Banana Bread French Toast (p. 79), or slice, toast and butter it on its own.

· ·

8 1/2 x 4 1/2-inch loaf pan (9 x 5-inch pan can be used)
Vegetable oil spray
1/2 pound ripe bananas, cut into 2-inch pieces
    (about 1 1/2 bananas)
1/2 cup sugar
1/2 cup light brown sugar
6 tablespoons butter
1 teaspoon salt
1 tablespoon baking soda
2 cups cake flour
1/2 cup water
2 eggs
1 teaspoon banana extract

Preheat the oven to 350°F. Cut a piece of parchment paper to fit the bottom of the loaf pan. Grease the loaf pan with vegetable oil spray. Place the paper in the bottom of pan. Grease the paper. Set aside.

Place the bananas, sugar, brown sugar, butter, salt, baking powder, and cake flour in a mixing bowl. Mix on low for about 2 minutes until the ingredients are combined.

Add the water and mix on medium speed for 2 minutes. With the mixer running, add the eggs and banana extract. Mix for 4 minutes. Spoon into the loaf pan. Bake for 1 hour.

Mango Bread

MAKES 10 TO 12 SLICES

From June through August, brightly colored mangoes hang from the trees around South Florida. Chef Tony Glitz from Alma Restaurant at the Hawks Cay Resort on Duck Key uses them in many ways. Here's his mango bread. It's delicious on its own and he also uses it for his Mango Bread Pudding (p. 230).

Mangoes can be found in most markets year-round. Mango puree and cubes are also sold frozen and work well for the recipe. If mangoes aren't available, use fresh pineapple.

• •

9 x 5-inch loaf pan
Vegetable oil spray
3/4 cup canola oil
3 eggs
1 1/2 cups sugar
2 cups all-purpose flour
3/4 cup whole-wheat flour
1 teaspoon baking soda
1 teaspoon salt
6 tablespoons mango puree
1 1/4 cups chopped mango

Preheat the oven to 325°F. Grease a 9 x 5-inch loaf pan with vegetable oil spray. Cut a piece of parchment paper or foil to fit the bottom of the pan and grease the paper. Mix the oil, eggs, and sugar together until smooth. Add the all-purpose flour, whole-wheat flour, baking soda, and salt. Mix well. Add the mango puree and chopped mango. Mix until combined. Spoon the batter into the loaf pan. Bake for 1 hour. Cover the top of the pan with foil to keep the bread from becoming too brown on top. Continue to bake for 30 minutes or until the bread is done. A cake tester or toothpick will come out clean. Remove from the oven, run a knife along the edges, and turn out onto a cake rack to cool. Can be frozen.

Avocado Bread

MAKES 10 TO 12 SLICES

When large, buttery avocados come into season in the Keys, everyone starts looking for new ways to use their backyard crops. Gerri Richman loves to bake and gave me this recipe. She and her husband used to have a restaurant in Key Largo. They've sold it and moved on. This is a great way to use any type of ripe avocado.

• •

9 x 5-inch loaf pan
Vegetable oil spray
3/4 cup mashed ripe avocado
3 eggs
1 cup vegetable oil
3 teaspoons vanilla
3 cups all-purpose flour
1 1/2 cups sugar
2 teaspoons cinnamon
1 teaspoon baking soda
1/2 teaspoon baking powder
3/4 cup chopped walnuts

Preheat the oven to 350°F. Grease the loaf pan with vegetable oil spray and set aside.

Mix the mashed avocado, eggs, oil, and vanilla together in a large bowl. Blend well. Add the flour, sugar, cinnamon, baking soda, and baking powder and stir to combine. Fold in the nuts and spoon into the prepared pan. Bake for 30 minutes. Cover the top loosely with foil to prevent burning. Bake for 1 hour more.

Cheeca Monkey Bread

SERVES 10

The aroma of this monkey bread baking will bring family and friends running to the kitchen. Cinnamon, sugar, macadamia nuts, and bananas coat the biscuit segments, and a guava cream-cheese frosting tops the bread. It's perfect for breakfast or brunch or just on its own.

Chef David Matlock created this recipe for Cheeca Lodge and Spa. It's easy to make using refrigerated biscuit dough. Each biscuit piece is coated with cinnamon and sugar. When the bread is baked, the coated pieces form segments that are easy to pull apart. Serve the bread warm.

• •

1 8- to 9-inch tube pan
Vegetable oil spray
1/4 cup sugar
2 tablespoons ground cinnamon
3 12-ounce cans refrigerated biscuits (30 biscuits)
1/4 cup chopped macadamia nuts
1 small sliced banana — not too ripe
1/2 cup packed brown sugar
6 tablespoons butter

Preheat the oven to 350°F and grease an 8- to 9-inch tube pan with vegetable oil spray. Mix the white sugar and cinnamon in a medium-size plastic bag. Open the biscuit tubes and remove the biscuits. Cut the biscuits into halves. Place six to eight biscuit pieces in the sugar-cinnamon mix in the bag and shake well. Arrange the pieces in the bottom of the greased pan. Coat the remaining biscuit pieces with sugar and cinnamon in the same manner. Continue layering the biscuit pieces, sprinkling the macadamia nuts and banana slices among the pieces as you layer them. The pan should be 3/4 filled. Do not overfill the pan. In a small saucepan, melt the butter with the brown sugar over medium heat. Boil for 1 minute. Pour over the layered biscuits. Bake for 40 minutes and remove from the oven. Let the bread cool in the pan for 10 minutes, then turn out onto a plate. Let cool for about 10 minutes more before adding the icing.

Monkey Bread Icing

2 ounces cream cheese
4 tablespoons butter
Vegetable oil spray
1/4 cup guava paste
1 cup confectioners' sugar
1/4 teaspoon vanilla extract
1/4 teaspoon lemon juice

Allow the cream cheese and butter to come to room temperature. Spray a small saucepan with vegetable oil spray. Place over low heat and add the guava paste. Cook until the paste is soft and can be blended into the butter and cream cheese. Beat the butter, cream cheese, and heated guava paste together in an electric mixer. Slowly add in the confectioners' sugar. After all the sugar is added, mix for 12 minutes (do not shorten the time). When almost done, add in the vanilla extract and lemon juice. Spread over the warm bread.

Chayote

Chayote is a tropical squash that looks like a green gnarled pear and has been traced to the Aztec and Mayan cultures. It belongs to the squash and cucumber family and can be used in the same manner as these vegetables. It can be peeled and grated, boiled and stuffed, or sliced and used instead of water chestnuts in stir-fries. It can also be eaten raw. Use squash as a substitute.

Chorizo

A spicy Cuban sausage usually made from pork and liver. Any type of spicy sausage can be used as a substitute.

Clarified Butter

Clarified butter is made by melting butter and discarding the milk solids. To do this, heat 2 tablespoons butter until it foams. Pour into a bowl to cool. The sediment that falls to the bottom should be scraped away from the cooled fat, which has been "clarified." The clarified butter will keep for months in the refrigerator or freezer. It will also reach a high temperature without burning. You can use 1 tablespoon oil and 1 tablespoon butter as a substitute. It will reach a good sautéing temperature without burning.

Sweetened Condensed Milk

Sweetened condensed milk plays an important part in Keys cooking. It is not the same as evaporated milk, and the two are not interchangeable in recipes.

In an era when refrigeration was scarce and many cows were unhealthy and infected with disease, sweetened condensed milk was a major source of wholesome milk. In 1853, Gail Borden, considered the father of the modern dairy industry, perfected the method of extracting water from milk and adding sugar as a preservative. Sweetened condensed milk is a blend of whole milk and pure cane sugar with 60 percent of the water removed under vacuum. It has a thick, creamy consistency. Used to feed the Union Army during the Civil War, it was also popular for infant feeding until 1938, when doctors started prescribing baby formulas. During World War II, sweetened condensed milk was used in dessert recipes because sugar was scarce.

Sweetened condensed milk naturally thickens with the addition of an acid such as key lime juice.

Chimichurri Sauce

Chimichurri sauce is a traditional Latin dish. It usually contains parsley, cilantro, garlic, vinegar, oil, and hot pepper flakes. It's used as a condiment or marinade.

Evaporated Milk

Evaporated milk is whole milk with the water removed. No sugar has been added. It is not interchangeable in recipes with sweetened condensed milk. When an acid such as lemon or lime juice is mixed with evaporated milk, the milk curdles, making it unfit for use in such recipes as key lime pie.

Guava

Fresh guavas are round or oval fruits about the size of a small orange. They are a rich source of vitamin C. The flesh has an intense flavor and a meaty texture. The fruit is usually cooked because of its large pectin content; it can easily be made into a paste, which many cooks prefer. The paste can be found in cans or in long, narrow boxes in most supermarkets.

Key Lime

The shrubby key lime tree, *Citrus aurantifolia*, with its thorny branches grows to about fifteen feet tall. It is believed to have come from the sour orange tree and to have been brought to this hemisphere from the East Indies.

Some say that Dr. Henry Perrine, governor-general of Indian Key during the 1830s, brought the tree to the Keys from Mexico; others believe it was imported by the Spanish and planted in the eighteenth century. Whichever way it came, it flourished in the Keys climate. It grows true from seeds and does not need grafting.

Key limes are yellow and look like small lemons. A key lime pie should be very pale yellow and not green. When making a pie with true key limes, it will set immediately without any gelatin because of the high acid content of the lime. Most native key limes sold in the markets now come either from private homes or are imported from Mexico or parts of South America. Citrus canker and hurricanes greatly curtailed the South Florida crop. Persian limes or green limes can be substituted in the key lime recipes.

Key West Shrimp

Sometimes called pink gold, these pink-shelled, juicy large shrimp are the prize of the important Keys shrimping industry. They remain pink when cooked. They're delicious, and cooking with them produces wonderful recipes. Any good-quality large shrimp can be substituted in the recipes.

Mango

A native of southern Asia for at least four thousand years, the mango has been cultivated in South Florida since the early 1800s. Florida mangoes can weigh anywhere from a half a pound to several pounds apiece. There are now many varieties, all coming into season between May and September. Their flavor has been described as a blend of peach, apricot, and pineapple, but in reality, their rich flavor is all their own. Mangoes are wonderful just eaten plain. The cubed flesh is a great addition to chicken salads or as a complement to meat and vegetable dishes. Peaches may be used as a substitute in most recipes. Unripe mangoes make excellent chutneys.

To make mango cubes, hold the mango upright with the narrow side facing you. With a sharp knife, slice off each side of the mango as close to the seed as possible. Cut the skin off the section containing the seed and cut as much fruit as possible away from the seed. Hold the other two portions peel side down and score the fruit down to the peel in a tic-tac-toe fashion. Hold the scored portion with both hands and bend the peel backward. The cubes will stick up like porcupine needles. Draw your knife across the peel to remove the cubes. Repeat for the other portion. Serve the cubes or puree them.

Mile Markers (MM)

The Keys stretch for about 127 miles from the mainland to the tip of Key West. U.S. 1, also called the Overseas Highway, is used to travel the islands of the Florida Keys. Locations along the highway are expressed in mile-marker numbers. The railroad first placed mile markers, little white signs with green numbers, along the road with mile marker 0 in Key West and mile marker 105 in Key Largo. Today most places in the Keys are located by their mile-marker number.

Mojo

Mojo is a sauce that is used as a marinade or condiment in many Latin dishes. There are many varieties. It usually contains olive oil, a lot of garlic, onion, cumin, vinegar, and sour orange or lime juice. It's sold in many supermarkets in the sauce or ethnic section.

Old Bay

This seasoning is used for flavoring seafood, especially shellfish, and is often used to flavor many other dishes. It is typically a blend of celery salt, mustard, pepper, bay leaf, cloves, allspice, ginger, mace, cardamom, cassia, and paprika.

Old Sour

This sauce seems to be a native of Key West, where it is used sparingly as a condiment on fish or chicken. In Cuba, it is used as a marinade or in cooking. It was probably first made to use up key limes and to have a supply of the juice when the limes were out of season. To make it, add 1 tablespoon of salt to 2 cups of lime juice. Let sit for at least two weeks in the refrigerator. It will keep for several weeks. Some people like to make their old sour hot by adding 2 bird peppers to the sauce. These tiny red or green peppers are about 1 inch long and are very hot. Use any type of chili pepper or hot sauce for your old sour.

Papaya

Papaya, also known as pawpaw, has been part of the tropical diet for centuries. Christopher Columbus wrote in his journal that when he landed he noticed the natives of the West Indies eating a "tree melon" called "the fruit of the angels." It is a native of the Caribbean area and is grown in Florida. Papayas come in a variety of shapes and colors, the flesh ranging from pale yellow to golden orange. The Caribbean Sunrise strain has a rich red-orange color and has been developed so that it can be picked when nearly ripe. These have a flowery fragrance that makes the papaya a special treat. They are available year-round. When green, the papaya is boiled or cut in half and baked like squash. Ripe papayas can be pureed for dressings, cooked with meat and poultry, served in fruit salads, or poached for desserts. The papaya remains firm when cooked.

Plantain

The plantain is a member of the banana family and looks like an oversize banana. When they are green, they are hard and starchy and are used very much like a potato or sliced and fried for plantain chips or mariquitas. As they ripen, they turn yellow and then black and develop more of a sweet banana flavor, but they hold their shape better than bananas when cooked. Peeling a plantain is a little tricky, as the peel wants to stick to the flesh. Take a knife and slice the skin along the natural ridges of the plantain. Then peel the strips away. If you have a yellow plantain that is not quite ripe yet, place it in a 300°F oven until it turns black and the skin begins to split. This only works with plantains that have already started to turn yellow. Bananas can be substituted for plantains in recipes, but they are softer and should be handled carefully during cooking.

Ponzu Sauce

Ponzu sauce is used mostly in Japanese recipes. It is made with yuzu, a citrus fruit, and has a tart flavor. It can be bought in bottles in many supermarkets.

Yuzu

Yuzu is an Asian citrus fruit. It's tart and tastes like a mixture of grapefruit and orange flavors. If you can't find yuzu, 2 tablespoons lime juice mixed with 1/2 tablespoon honey will work well as a substitute.

Wasabi Powder

Wasabi powder is a variety of green horseradish grown only in Japan. It has a sharp flavor and is a little hotter than white horseradish. It provides heat to a dish and also an herbal overtone. Combine equal parts wasabi powder with water to use in recipes. The powder can be found in many supermarkets.

Keys Restaurants

KEY LARGO

Alabama Jack's
58000 Card Sound Road
Key Largo, FL 33037
305-248-8741
www.alabamajacks.com

Ballyhoo's Seafood Grille
97860 Overseas Highway
MM 97.8, In the Median
Key Largo, FL 33037
305-852-0822
www.ballyhoorestaurant.com

Doc's Diner
Jim Boilini
99696 Overseas Highway
MM 99.7
Key Largo, FL 33037
305-451-2895
www.docsdinerkeylargo.com

The Fish House Restaurant and Fish Market
102401 Overseas Highway
MM 102.3
Key Largo, FL 33037
305-451- HOOK (4665)
888-451-HOOK (4665)
www.fishhouse.com

The Fish House Encore Restaurant and Sushi Bar
102341 Overseas Highway
MM 102.5 Oceanside
Key Largo, FL 33037
305-451-0650
www.fishhouse.com

Gilbert's Tiki Bar and Resort and Marina
107900 Overseas Highway
MM 107.9
Key Largo, FL 33037
305-451-1133
www.gilbertsresort.com

The Key Largo Conch House
10021 Overseas Highway
MM100.2 Oceanside
Key Largo, FL 33037
305-453-4844
www.keylargocoffeehouse.com

Key Largo Fisheries
Dottie Hill
1313 Ocean Bay Drive
Key Largo, FL 33037
305-451-3782
www.keylargofisheries.com

Mrs. Mac's Kitchen
99336 Overseas Highway
MM 99.3
Key Largo, FL 33037
305-451-3722
www.mrsmacskitchen.com

Senor Frijoles
103900 Overseas Highway #B
MM 103.9
Key Largo, FL 33037
305-451-1592
www.senorfrijolesrestaurant.com

Sundowners
103900 Overseas Highway
MM 103.9
Key Largo, FL 33037-2816
305-451-5566
www.sundownerskeylargo.com

ISLAMORADA

Bentley's Restaurant
82779 Overseas Highway
MM 82.7
Islamorada, FL 33036-3609
305-664-9094

Cheeca Lodge and Spa
81801 Overseas Highway
MM 82
Islamorada, FL 33036
305-664-4651
www.cheeca.com

City Hall Café
John Bedell owner
MM 88.5 Oceanside
Islamorada, FL 33070
305-852-DELI
www.cityhallcafe.net

Debbiy Doo's Deli and Market Fresh
82229 Overseas Highway
MM 82.2
Islamorada, FL 33036-3659
305-664-8847

Green Turtle Inn
81219 Overseas Highway
MM 81.2
Islamorada, FL 33036
305-664-2006
www.greenturtlekeys.com

Holiday Isle Resort and Marina
84001 Overseas Highway
MM 84 Oceanside
Islamorada, FL 33036
305-664-2321
www.holidayisle.com

Island Grill
85501 Overseas Highway
MM 85.5
Islamorada, FL 33036
305-664-8400
www.keysislandgrill.com

Islamorada Bakery and Bob's Bunz
81620 Overseas Highway
MM 81.6
Islamorada, FL 33036
305-664-8363
www.bobsbunz.com

Islamorada Fish Company
81532 Overseas Highway
MM 81.5
Islamorada, FL 33037
305-664-9271
www.fishcompany.com

Kaiyo Restaurant
81701 Old Highway
MM 81.7
Islamorada, FL 33036
305-664-2888
www.kaiyokeys.com

Lazy Days Restaurant
Lupe Ledesma
79867 Overseas Highway
MM 79.9
Islamorada, FL 33036
305-664-5256
www.lazydaysrestaurant.com

Lorelei Restaurant and Cabana Bar
81924 Overseas Highway
MM 81.9
Islamorada, FL 33036
305-664-2692
www.loreleifloridakeys.com

MA's Fish Camp
105 Palm Avenue
MM 81.5 Oceanside
Islamorada, FL 33036
305-517-9611

Marker 88 Restaurant
87900 Overseas Highway
MM 88 Bayside
Islamorada, FL 33036-3050
(305) 852-9315
www.marker88.info

Midway Café and Coffee Bar
80499 Overseas Highway
MM 80.4
Islamorada, FL 33036
305-664-2622

On the Bricks Café
81905 Overseas Highway
MM 81.9
Islamorada, FL 33036
786-226-6516

Pierre's and Morada Bay Beach Café
81600 Overseas Highway
MM 81.6
Islamorada, FL 33036
305-664-3225
Pierre's Morada Bay
305-664-0604
www.pierres-restaurant.com

Spanish Gardens and Café
Jose Palomino
80925 Overseas Highway #10
MM 80.9 Oceanside
Islamorada, FL 33036
305-664-3999
www.spanishgardenscafe.com

DUCK KEY

Hawks Cay Resort and Marina
Alma Restaurant
Beach Grill
Tom's Harbor House
61 Hawks Cay Boulevard
MM 61
Duck Key, FL 33050
305-743-7000
888-313-5749
www.hawkscay.com

CUDJOE KEY

Square Grouper Bar and Grill
22658 Overseas Highway
MM 22.5
Cudjoe Key, FL 33042
305-745-8880

Zane Grey Long Key Lounge
81576 Overseas Highway
MM 81.5
Islamorada, FL 33036
305-664-4244

Ziggie and Mad Dog's
83000 Overseas Highway
MM 83 Bayside
Islamorada, FL 33036
305-664-3391
www.ziggieandmaddogs.com

LITTLE TORCH KEY

Little Palm Island Resort and Spa
28500 Overseas Highway
Little Torch Key, FL 33042
800-343-8567
800-3-GET LOST
www.littlepalmisland.com

KEY WEST

A & B Lobster House
700 Front Street
Key West, FL 33040
305-294-5880
www.aandblobsterhouse.com

Azur Restaurant
425 Grinnell Street
Key West, FL 33040
305-292-2987
www.azurkeywest.com

Banana Café
1215 Duval Street
Key West, FL 33040
305-294-7227
www.bananacafekw.com

Blue Heaven
729 Thomas Street
Key West, FL 33040
305-296-8666
www.blueheavenkw.com

Bo's Fish Wagon
801 Caroline Street
Key West, FL 33140
305-294-9272
www.bofishwagon.com

The Café at the Inn at Key West
3420 Roosevelt Boulevard (U.S. 1)
Key West, FL 33040
305-330-5541
www.theinnatkeywest.com

Café Sole
1029 Southard Sreet
Key West, FL 33040
305-294-0230
www.cafesole.com

Cole's Peace
1111 Eaton Street
Key West, FL 33040
305-292-0703
www.colespeace.com

Eaton Street Seafood Market
801 Eaton Street
Key West, FL 33040
305-295-FISH (3474)
www.kwseafood.com

Finnegan's Wake
320 Grinnell Street
Key West, FL 33040
305-797-5668
www.keywestirish.com

Grand Café
314 Duval Street
Key West, FL 33040
305-292-4740
www.grandcafekeywest.com

Help Yourself
829 Fleming Street
Key West, FL 33040
305-296-7766
www.helpyourselffoods.com

Hog's Breath Saloon
400 Front Street
Key West, FL 33040
305-292-2032
www.hogsbreath.com/key-west

Hogfish Bar and Grill
6810 Front Street
Stock Island, FL 33040
305-293-4041
www.hogfishbar.com

Key West Marriott Beachside Hotel
3841 North Roosevelt Boulevard
Key West, FL 33040
800-546-0885
www.beachsidekeywest.com

Louie's Backyard
700 Waddel Avenue
Key West, FL 33040
305-294-1061
www.louiesbackyard.com

Margaritaville Key West
500 Duval Street
Key West, FL 33040
305-292-1435
www.margaritavillekeywest.com

Michaels
532 Margaret Street
Key West, FL 33040
305-295-1300
www.michaelskeywest.com

Martin's on Duval
917 Duval Street
Key West, FL 33040
305-294-5602
www.martinskeywest.com

Nine One Five Duval
915 Duval Street
Key West, FL 33040
305-296-0669
www.915duval.com

Pepe's Café
806 Caroline Street
Key West, FL 33040
305-294-7192
www.pepescafe.net

Santiago's Bodega
207 Petronia Street
Key West, FL 33040
305-296-7691
www.santiagosbodega.com

Salute
1000 Atlantic Boulevard
Key West, FL 33040
305-292-1117
www.saluteonthebeach.com

Small Chef at Large
    (White Street Bistro)
1019 White Street
Key West, FL 33040
305-294-1943
www.smallchefatlarge.com

Sarabeth's Key West
530 Simmington Street
Key West, FL 33040
305-293-8181
www.sarabethskeywest.com

Sloppy Joe's
201 Duval Street
Key West, FL 33040
305-296-2388
www.sloppyjoes.com

Acknowledgments

Traveling through the Florida Keys is a special experience. I loved meeting the people, gathering their stories, and experiencing their food. Their diversity and history make the Florida Keys a very special place. Thank you to all of the people who helped me along the way.

My biggest thank-you goes to my husband, Harold, who encouraged me, helped me test every recipe, washed the dishes, and spent hours helping me edit every word. His constant support for all of my work has made this book a partnership.

Thank you to Simon Hallgarten, one of the parteners of Northview Hotel Group LLC, which owns Hawks Cay Resort, who supported and encouraged this project and enabled it to come to fruition.

To everyone at the beautiful Hawks Cay resort and Marina: Sheldon Suga, managing director, Chef Wolfgang Birk, Chef Reto von Weissenfluh, Jennifer Dinan, and Shay Onorio. Thank you for introducing us to the Hawks Cay experience, hosting us, helping with the book photos, and working tirelessly to help capture the flavors of the Florida Keys.

Many thanks to Eric Price, my editor at Grove/Atlantic, whose enthusiasm for the Florida Keys added enormously to this book and made this project a pleasure, and to Charles Woods, art director at Grove/Atlantic, who captured the essence of the Keys through his camera lens and whose design helped bring this book to life.

Kitty Clement introduced me to everyone she knew in Key West and guided me around her town. Many thanks to Kitty and to her husband, Tom, who waited patiently for us to taste, interview, and record, and smiled through it all.

Thank you to my friends Chef Jean Pierre and Diane LeJeune, who helped me seek out the best of Islamorada. Their expert advice was a wonderful beacon.

Lisa Ekus, my long-time friend and agent inspired me to create this book.

Thank you to my *Miami Herald* editor, Kathy Martin, for her constant support of my "Dinner in Minutes" column, as well as this and other projects.

Thank you to Joseph Cooper, host of "Topical Currents," and to the staff at WLRN National Public Radio for their help with and enthusiasm for my weekly "Food News and Views" segment, and their constant support and enthusiasm for this and my other projects.

I'd also like to thank my family, who have always supported my projects and encouraged me every step of the way: my son James, his wife, Patty, and their children Zachary, Jacob, and Haley, who tasted recipes and gave their advice; my son, John, his wife, Jill, and their children, Jeffrey and Joanna, who cheered me on; my son Charles, his wife, Lori, and their sons, Daniel and Matthew, for their guidance; and my sister, Roberta, and brother-in-law, Robert, who provide a continuous sounding board for my ideas.

And, finally, many thanks to all of the chefs whose time and recipe contributions made this book possible. A list of their restaurants can be found on p. 255. I hope this sampling of their fare will tempt you to visit them.

Index